Traffic Signs Manual

Chapter 4

Warning Signs

Department for Transport

Department for Infrastructure (Northern Ireland)

Scottish Government

Welsh Government

London: TSO

Traffic Signs Manual

Contents of Chapters 1–8

* To be published at a later date

Designers should consult the Department for Transport's website www.gov.uk for confirmation of current publication dates.

Published for The Department for Transport under licence from the Controller of Her Majesty's Stationery Office

First published 2018
First edition Crown Copyright 1997

ISBN 978 0 11 553609 0

Printed In the United Kingdom for TSO (The Stationery Office)
J003507294   c2   11/18

CONTENTS

1 INTRODUCTION

1.1 General

1.1.1. The Traffic Signs Manual (the Manual) offers advice to traffic authorities and their contractors, designers and managing agents in the United Kingdom, on the use of traffic signs and road markings on the highway network. Mandatory requirements are set out in the Traffic Signs Regulations and General Directions 2016 (as amended) (TSRGD). In Northern Ireland the relevant legislation is the Traffic Signs Regulations (Northern Ireland) 1997 (as amended). Whilst the Manual can assist with complying with the mandatory requirements, it cannot provide a definitive legal interpretation, nor can it override them. This remains the prerogative of the courts or parking adjudicators in relation to the appearance and use of specific traffic signs, road markings etc. at specific locations.

1.1.2. The advice is given to assist authorities in the discharge of their duties under section 122 of the Road Traffic Regulation Act 1984 and Part 2 of the Traffic Management Act 2004 in England and under Part 1 of the Roads (Scotland) Act 1984. Subject to compliance with the Directions, which are mandatory (see **1.4.2** and **1.4.3**), it is for traffic authorities to determine what signing is necessary to meet those duties.

1.1.3. The Manual applies to the United Kingdom. References to "the national authority" should therefore be interpreted as referring to the Secretary of State for Transport, the Department for Infrastructure (Northern Ireland), the Scottish Government or the Welsh Government as appropriate. Any reference to the "Department" is a reference to the Department for Transport or the appropriate national authority for Northern Ireland, Scotland or Wales as described above.

1.1.4. This chapter of the Manual explains the use of the warning signs prescribed by TSRGD. It enables the correct sign to be used, and advises on the appropriate size and siting to ensure adequate warning of the hazard. Where markings are used to supplement upright signs or placed in connection with traffic signals and pedestrian crossings, guidance on these can be found in the following chapters:

a) Stop and Give Way markings: Chapter 3
b) Signal controlled junctions: Chapter 6
c) Pedestrian crossings: Chapter 6
d) Cycle markings: Chapter 3
e) Bus markings: Chapter 3
f) Tram markings: Chapter 3
g) Control of on street parking: Chapter 3
h) Markings associated with regulatory signs: Chapter 3

1.2 Legal

1.2.1. All road markings and road studs placed on a highway or on a road to which the public has access (right of passage in Scotland), as defined in section 142 of the Road Traffic Regulation Act 1984 and amended by the New Roads and Street Works Act 1991, must be either prescribed by Regulations or authorised by the Secretary of State for Transport (for installations in England), the Department for Infrastructure (Northern Ireland), the Scottish Government or the Welsh Government as appropriate.

1.2.2. There could be circumstances where it might be appropriate to use prescribed signs and markings in a manner that is not strictly in accordance with the General Directions or the Schedule-specific Directions. In such cases, a special direction (not an authorisation), given in writing, should be sought from the appropriate national authority. Signs, markings and road studs may be placed only by, or with the permission of, the traffic authority.

1.2.3. Occasionally a sign that is not prescribed by the Regulations may be authorised by the national authority for placing on a public highway.

1.3 Definitions

1.3.1. In the Manual, the word "must" is used to indicate a legal requirement of the Traffic Signs Regulations and General Directions (or other legislation) that must be complied with. The word "should" indicates a course of action that is recommended and represents good practice. The word "may" generally indicates a permissible action, or an option that requires consideration depending on the circumstances.

1.3.2. Section 64 of the Road Traffic Regulation Act 1984 defines a traffic sign as "any object or device (whether fixed or portable) for conveying to traffic on roads or any specified class of traffic, warnings, information, requirements, restrictions or prohibitions of any description … and any line or mark on the road for so conveying such warnings, information, requirements, restrictions or prohibitions" and stipulates that these signs be "specified by regulations made by the national authority, or authorised by the national authority". The types of signs and carriageway markings and their appropriate use are prescribed in TSRGD.

1.3.3. "Signing" includes not only traffic signs mounted on supports (and other structures such as gantries, bridges, railings, etc.) but also carriageway markings, beacons, studs, bollards, traffic signals, matrix signals and other devices prescribed in TSRGD.

1.4 References

1.4.1. Any reference to the "Regulations" or the "Directions" is a reference to the Traffic Signs Regulations and General Directions 2016, applicable to England, Scotland and Wales. Reference to a diagram number or to a Schedule is a reference to a diagram or Schedule in those Regulations.

1.4.2. In Northern Ireland, the relevant legislation is the Traffic Signs Regulations (Northern Ireland) 1997 as amended. Diagram numbering occasionally differs in these Regulations and references to Schedules do not apply to Northern Ireland. The design of road markings, meanings and permitted variants are generally similar but can vary; where the Northern Ireland Regulations apply, the designer is advised to read them in conjunction with the Manual.

1.4.3. Not all road markings referred to in the text are included in the Northern Ireland Regulations. References to directions are not applicable in Northern Ireland; where these are referred to, advice should be sought from the Department for Infrastructure's Headquarters.

1.5 Format

1.5.1. Any reference to a "Chapter" is a reference to a Chapter of the Traffic Signs Manual, and any reference to a "section", unless otherwise stated, is a reference to a section within a chapter of the Manual. Where more detailed background information might be helpful, reference is made to Standards and Advice Notes in the Design Manual for Roads and Bridges (DMRB), published by TSO and available at:

www.standardsforhighways.co.uk/dmrb

1.5.2. References to Schedules, Parts, items and paragraphs within TSRGD are shown in an abbreviated format. In this system, "Schedule" is shortened to "S" and "Part" is indicated by the second number without a prefix. The final element, variously "item" or "paragraph" is also denoted by a number without a prefix. This is illustrated in the following examples:

1.5.3. "Schedule 9, Part 6, item 25" becomes "S9-6-25"

1.5.4. "Schedule 11, Part 6, paragraph 3" becomes "S11-6-3"

1.5.5. "Schedule 12, Part 2" becomes "S12-2"

1.5.6. The numbering system contained in the Manual utilises three levels comprising sections, sub-headings and numbered paragraphs. Internal references are in **bold blue**.

1.6 Use of warning signs

1.6.1. Warning signs are used to alert drivers to potential danger ahead. They indicate a need for special caution by road users and may require a reduction in speed or some other manoeuvre.

1.6.2. Warning signs can play an important part in improving road safety. However, they should only be used where there is a specific safety issue or hazard, not to sign readily apparent conditions or routine features of the road, such as bends and junctions. Overuse of warning signs can dilute their effectiveness and tends to bring them into disrepute. For example, it should not be necessary to place roundabout or traffic signal warning signs in addition to map-type advanced direction signs or where the traffic signals or roundabout are clearly visible. Similarly, junction warning signs should not be necessary in street-lit urban areas, where there are frequent side-road junctions. Local authorities should work with local communities where specific issues and concerns are raised, to make sure the right solution is found. Warning signs should only be installed where there is an identified hazard or road safety problem, and not to solely meet a perceived need. Unjustified signing should not be used at individual locations simply in response to complaints from the public. Care should be taken to ensure that a route is treated consistently, especially where it crosses the boundary between two traffic authorities.

1.6.3. Certain warning signs may be incorporated into directional signs; for further details see Chapter 7.

1.6.4. Detailed guidance on the use of warning signs at road works is given in Chapter 8, and for the approach to signalled junctions and crossings in Chapter 6.

1.6.5. To prevent the proliferation of obsolete signs, and clutter, Schedule 13 stipulates that the temporary sign to diagram 7014 "NEW ROUNDABOUT AHEAD" (S13-6-37) and its variants, and the sign to diagram 790 "NEW LEVEL CROSSING AHEAD" (S14-2-67) must only be displayed for a maximum period of three months after completion of works. A remove by date must be placed on the back of the sign. See also **1.15.1** and section **7**.

1.7 Vehicle-activated signs

1.7.1. S2-7-3 permits certain warning signs (diagrams 504.1, 505.1, 506.1, 507.1, 510, 512, 512.1, 512.2, 512.3 and 513) when displayed by means of light-emitting characters or symbols also to display below the sign, and at the same time, the legend "SLOW DOWN" in characters not less than one quarter of the height of the triangle. The signs will be triggered by vehicles exceeding a pre-determined safe speed on the approach to a junction or bend. They should be used only to supplement fixed signing, and not as a substitute for it. Vehicle- activated signs should not be considered until the fixed signing and road markings have been checked to ensure that they comply fully with the guidance in this chapter and in Chapter 5 in terms of correct size, siting, visibility and condition.

1.8 Sign sizes

1.8.1. Warning signs are normally prescribed in five sizes. The normal minimum size is indicated in the Schedule diagram by the first dimension, with alternative sizes below. All sizes are in millimetres unless stated otherwise. Signs need to be of a size appropriate to the prevailing traffic speed on the road on which they are used. On roads with a 30 mph speed limit, the smallest prescribed size of warning triangle (normally 600 mm) is usually adequate. On roads where speeds are higher, signs need to be larger. This enables them to be detected at a greater distance and ensures that drivers have sufficient time to recognise and assimilate the warning and take any necessary action before the hazard is met. The largest signs are for use on motorways or high-speed roads. Appendix A details the appropriate size of sign for various speed ranges, based on the 85th percentile approach speed.

1.8.2. Where special amenity considerations apply, or there are physical constraints on the width of sign that can be accommodated, the next smaller size can be substituted. It should however be borne in mind that smaller signs are likely to be seen later, and do not become legible until drivers are closer to them, giving less time to react.

1.8.3. If the accident record suggests that drivers are failing to notice the warning, or seeing it too late to take the necessary action, the next larger size can be used. Conspicuity can also be increased by the use of yellow backing boards (see **1.12**). These are environmentally intrusive and should only be used sparingly, not as a matter of course.

1.8.4. Many warning signs are accompanied by supplementary plates. **Appendix B** recommends appropriate x-heights to match the size of the plates to the size of the triangle they are used with, and to ensure adequate legibility. There are restrictions on which plates may be used with individual signs and in some cases a plate is mandatory; the plates prescribed for use with each sign are indicated below each diagram illustrated in this Chapter. Detailed drawings showing the correct layouts for all permitted variants have been produced by the Department for Transport (see **1.16.1**).

1.8.5. A temporary sign (diagram 7014) is prescribed to warn drivers of a permanent change in the road layout ahead (see **1.6.5**). Several variants are prescribed, e.g. "GAP CLOSED AHEAD", "NEW TRAFFIC SIGNALS AHEAD" and "NEW ZEBRA CROSSING AHEAD". The x-height of the sign may vary between 50 and 200 mm (i.e. the capital letter height varies between 70 and 280 mm). The appropriate x-height at a specific site will depend upon the speed of traffic, with the 50 mm x-height suitable for speeds up to 30 mph and 150 or 200 mm for 70 mph. Intermediate sizes should be used for speeds between these extremes.

1.9 Siting

1.9.1. In general, the greater the speed of approach, the further in advance of the hazard the sign needs to be placed. This is to ensure that drivers have the necessary time to respond to the warning. **Appendix A** sets out recommendations for the distance from the hazard at which a sign should be sited. If it is impracticable to place a sign within about 10% of the recommended distance, it should be sited further upstream of the hazard at the nearest practicable point. It may be appropriate to supplement it with a distance plate (see section **17**). A sign should not normally be sited more than 10% closer than the recommended distance, as this would be unlikely to provide sufficient warning. Where this is unavoidable, a distance plate should always be used, indicating the distance to the hazard to the nearest 10 yards.

1.9.2. Warning signs should normally be placed on the left hand side of the road, unless stated otherwise in the text (e.g. hazard markers to diagram 560, S2-6-2). However, site conditions sometimes make this impracticable. A warning sign might be placed on the right hand side on a left hand bend if it would otherwise be hidden from view, or if there would be no room for it on the left. If a sign is placed on the right hand side of the road, care must be taken to ensure that a driver would not be misled at night or in fog as to which side to pass. It might sometimes be appropriate to duplicate warning signs by providing them on each side of the road, as is recommended at the end of a dual carriageway, or on the approach to a roundabout on a high-speed road.

1.9.3. It is essential that drivers have an unobstructed view of traffic signs. The distance which should be kept clear of obstructions to the sight line, whether caused by foliage, other signs or street furniture, is known as the clear visibility distance. The higher the prevailing traffic speeds, the greater this distance needs to be. It is important therefore that sight lines are properly maintained so that the intended warning is not compromised. Care in siting can minimise future problems of obscuration. Sight lines should not cross private land as it will be difficult to control the growth of vegetation or the placement of other obstructions. It is equally important that warning signs should not be placed where they will obstruct the view of other signs e.g. advance direction signs. Such problems might be avoided by siting the sign further from the hazard, or on the right hand side of the road.

1.9.4. **Appendix A** recommends minimum clear visibility distances. These should normally be measured from the centre of the most disadvantaged driving lane. It is important that the full recommended sight line to the whole of the sign face is preserved. Trimming of foliage only in the immediate vicinity of the sign may not be sufficient; sign visibility should always be checked from the appropriate viewing distance.

1.10 Mounting

1.10.1. The normal mounting height measured to the lower edge of a warning sign is between 900 mm and 1500 mm above the carriageway alongside. The greater height should be used where road spray is likely to soil the sign. Where signs are erected above footways, or in areas likely or intended to be used by pedestrians (e.g. pedestrian refuges), a minimum headroom of 2300 mm is recommended, with 2100 mm as an absolute minimum. A clearance of 2400 mm should be maintained over a cycle track or shared cycle track/footway. When supplementary plates are used, the height should be measured to the bottom of the plate.

1.10.2. Plates should be separated from the sign or another plate by a vertical space not exceeding the x-height of the lettering.

1.10.3. Except where they support a luminaire, posts should not project above the top of the sign. This practice is unsightly, and needlessly increases visual intrusion and clutter.

1.11 Mounting more than one sign on a post

1.11.1. Research has shown that the greater the number of signs which drivers are presented with simultaneously, the greater the difficulty they are likely to have in assimilating the information. This problem in dealing with information overload increases with age, so that older drivers suffer disproportionately. Generally, therefore, not more than two signs should be mounted on one post. When a sign is accompanied by a supplementary plate, the combination of sign and plate should be regarded as one sign for this purpose. Exceptionally, three signs may be mounted on one post provided none requires a supplementary plate.

1.11.2. Warning signs should not be mounted on the same post as a STOP or GIVE WAY or terminal speed limit sign, nor mounted on a traffic signal post. When mounted with other types of sign, the triangular warning signs should always be mounted at the top.

1.11.3. Where two or more warning signs are erected together, the sign relating to the hazard first encountered should be placed uppermost. When a new sign is added to an existing post, a review of current signs should be carried out, and if all are still required it is important to ensure that the correct order is maintained, if necessary adjusting the position of the existing signs.

1.11.4. Generally no assembly should exceed a height of 4 m above ground level. All proposed assemblies should be critically examined to ensure that the intended warnings are clear. Account should always be taken of the potential environmental impact of tall and cluttered arrays of signs.

1.11.5. It should also be borne in mind that high-mounted signs may receive little light from vehicle headlamps, particularly on dipped beam. Where such signs are not directly lit but rely on reflectorisation to be seen at night, they are likely to be less legible (see also **2.4**).

1.12 Backing boards

1.12.1. To improve conspicuity against a complex or dark background, a warning sign may be mounted on a grey or yellow backing board (direction 9). A backing board can also make for a neater assembly, e.g. when a sign requires a supplementary plate, and also eliminates the risk of the plate becoming misaligned. A yellow backing board must be rectangular (including square) in shape, but a grey one may be non-rectangular. A backing board must not itself be provided with a border, nor give the impression of being an additional border. Where it seems that a sign is not being noticed by drivers, it should be checked to ensure that it is well-sited, not obscured by foliage or other obstructions, and is of the appropriate size and in good condition. Only then should the use of a yellow backing board be considered. They should be used very sparingly and not as a matter of course.

1.12.2. A yellow backing board may be reflectorised to increase its conspicuity at night. This should not usually be necessary on unlit roads, although it might sometimes be helpful on lit roads, particularly where the sign itself is unlit. It may also be fluorescent; this greatly increases conspicuity in dull weather and at dusk. Fluorescence can also be particularly effective in drawing attention to signs mounted in deep shadow, e.g. below overhanging trees. However, fluorescence is visually intrusive and should be used with discretion.

1.12.3. There are potential disadvantages to the use of backing boards. The larger overall size of the assembly can sometimes obstruct sight lines. A backing board can deprive triangular signs of a primary recognition aid; their distinctive silhouette. Yellow backing boards are environmentally intrusive, and their over-use could eventually devalue their attention-attracting benefits. A less garish way of increasing a sign's conspicuity is simply to provide a standard sign of larger size. Not only will this be more noticeable than a smaller sign, but it will also improve legibility and hence reading distance, which a yellow backing board cannot. Detailed guidance on the correct design and use of backing boards can be found in Chapter 7.

1.13 Illumination

1.13.1. On unlit roads, reflectorisation generally produces an adequate level of sign luminance in the illumination from a vehicle's headlamps. In areas of street lighting, however, much higher levels of luminance are required to ensure that signs are always adequately conspicuous. Reflectorised materials cannot guarantee luminance levels comparable to those provided by direct lighting. Modern microprismatic materials may be specified. Some of these can achieve high luminances for many drivers in defined situations, but not for all drivers in all circumstances.

1.13.2. The warning signs to diagrams 501 (S2-6-1), 530A (S2-4-2), 531.1A (S2-4-3), 629.2A (S3-2-27), 770 (S2-2-51), 771 (S2-2-52), 772 (S2-2-53), 779 (S2-2-54) and 782 (S2-2-55) must be illuminated throughout the hours of darkness by internal or external lighting when sited within 50 metres of a street lamp which forms part of a system of street lighting unless within a 20 mph speed limit. In most other circumstances, reflectorisation alone will be satisfactory. However, some signs are sited where they will not receive adequate illumination from headlamps, and it might then be prudent to provide internal or external lighting regardless of the regulatory requirements. Examples include signs mounted unusually high above the level of the carriageway, or on the off side of the road. Retroreflection is also less effective where the sign is presented at a large angle to the direction of oncoming traffic.

1.13.3. Illumination requirements for upright traffic signs and road markings are set out in regulations 8 and 9 respectively, and, where appropriate, in individual Schedules. Most warning signs are required to be illuminated in accordance with regulation 8. This allows a simple alternative between reflectorisation and internal or external lighting, although they may be lit by both, wherever the sign is sited. It is recommended that an assessment of required performance is carried out to determine the best retroreflective material for the location where a sign is reflectorised instead of being internally or externally lit. Materials that offer performance little better than conventional beaded sheetings are unlikely to be adequate.

1.13.4. All warning signs, including those used at street works and road works must therefore be either reflectorised or internally or externally lit, except for the overhead black and yellow hazard markings and white chord markings used on railway bridges and similar structures, where this is optional. It is recommended that signs that are internally or externally lit are also reflectorised in order to maintain some degree of illumination in the event of failure of the lighting. Where a sign is reflectorised, all parts of the sign face not coloured black must be reflectorised (regulation 8). Partial reflectorisation is unlawful, as is partial lighting.

1.14 Maintenance

1.14.1. Over a period of years, signs gradually become faded and their retroreflective properties diminish. This will reduce both conspicuity and legibility, by day and by night. Excessively discoloured or faded signs (e.g. white backgrounds which have become grey or brown, or red borders faded to pink) and signs where the legend or graphic is peeling cannot be fully effective and need to be replaced. Guidance can be found in TD 25, in Volume 8 of DMRB (see 1.5.1).

1.14.2. Signs should be cleaned at intervals appropriate to the site conditions. Signs located where they are subject to heavy soiling from passing traffic, or algae growth (a common problem for signs beneath tree canopies) will need more frequent cleaning. Neglect reduces the external contrast between the sign and its surroundings, making it less likely to be noticed by drivers. It also reduces the internal contrast between legend and sign background, making the sign more difficult to read. Moreover, it seriously reduces light transmission through the retroreflective medium. Dirty signs are far less effective at night. Older drivers are particularly disadvantaged; the ageing process of the eye means that progressively more light is required to maintain the same legibility performance. Dimmer signs take longer to recognise and to read, reducing the time available for drivers to take appropriate action.

1.14.3. The importance of maintaining the necessary clear visibility distance is emphasised in 1.9.3 and 1.9.4. Regular inspection, particularly in summer when the rapid growth of foliage and other vegetation is most likely to cause obscuration, will ensure early detection of any problems.

1.14.4. A reference number may be placed on the back of a sign in a contrasting colour in characters not exceeding 25 mm in height, or embossed in the same colour in characters not exceeding 50 mm in height (direction 9). It is unlawful, as well as distracting and unsightly, to place reference numbers on the sign face or on the front of a backing board.

1.15 Temporary signs

1.15.1. Certain signs in S13-2 are intended to be displayed only during transient conditions. These include diagrams 551.1 (Migratory toad crossing, S13-2-1), 554A (Flood, S13-2-2), 554D (No smoking, S13-2-3), 554.2 (Ice, S13-2-4), 556 (Uneven road, S13-2-5), 557 (Slippery road, S13-2-6) and some applications of 562 with associated plate (Other danger, S13-2-7). They should be removed when the danger has passed. Diagram 7014 warns of a permanent change in road layout or new traffic signals etc. This sign must display a remove by date on the reverse, limited to a maximum period of three months after completion of the works (S13-7-8 and Direction 12). Such signs should be used sparingly and not as a matter of course. Diagram 7014.1 (S13-6-39) warns of a reduction in headroom at a bridge. Where this reduction is temporary, the sign may be retained only for the duration of the reduction. When a permanent reduction occurs, resulting in headroom of less than 16'-6" (5.03 m), the sign may be retained for a period of six months and must display a remove by date on the reverse (see 7.3.4). Authorities that fail to comply with their statutory responsibilities to remove redundant signs not only devalue the signs but contribute to sign clutter.

1.15.2. S13-9 permits a traffic authority to provide a temporary sign to warn of a temporary hazard caused by works being executed on a road, adverse weather conditions or other natural causes, the failure of street lighting or malfunction of or damage to other equipment used in connection with the road, or damage to the road itself. Schedule 13, Direction 16 requires such signs to be removed as soon as the hazard has passed, and in any case within six months.

1.15.3. A sign prescribed in the Regulations must be used where the warning can be conveyed by such a sign. Otherwise it may be designed following the requirements specified in S13-9. The back of a temporary sign must be grey, black or in a non-reflective metallic finish, as for almost all other signs (direction 9). The use of a yellow or other coloured back is unsightly, visually intrusive and unlawful.

1.16 Working drawings

1.16.1. Dimensions on the figures are in millimetres unless stated otherwise. Many markings are fully dimensioned in the Regulations. Detailed working drawings of the more complex ones are available at:

www.gov.uk/government/collections/traffic-signs-signals-and-road-markings

1.16.2. Workings drawings for Welsh and English bilingual signs are available at

www.traffic-wales.com/traffic_signs.aspx

2.1 General

2.1.1. The sign to diagram 501 (S2-6-1, see **Figure 2-1**) should be used where the clear visibility distance (see **1.9.3** and **1.9.4**) to the STOP or GIVE WAY sign is less than the distance given in **Table 2-1**. The sign may also be accompanied by the word SLOW (diagram 1024) marked on the carriageway. Where the junction is with a dual carriageway road, the "Dual carriageway" plate remains below the STOP or GIVE WAY plate (see also **5.6**). Where there is a gap in the central reservation and a right turn is permitted, this should reduce the risk of drivers turning into the wrong carriageway. See Chapter 3 for further guidance on the STOP and GIVE WAY signs, and Chapter 5 for road markings at junctions.

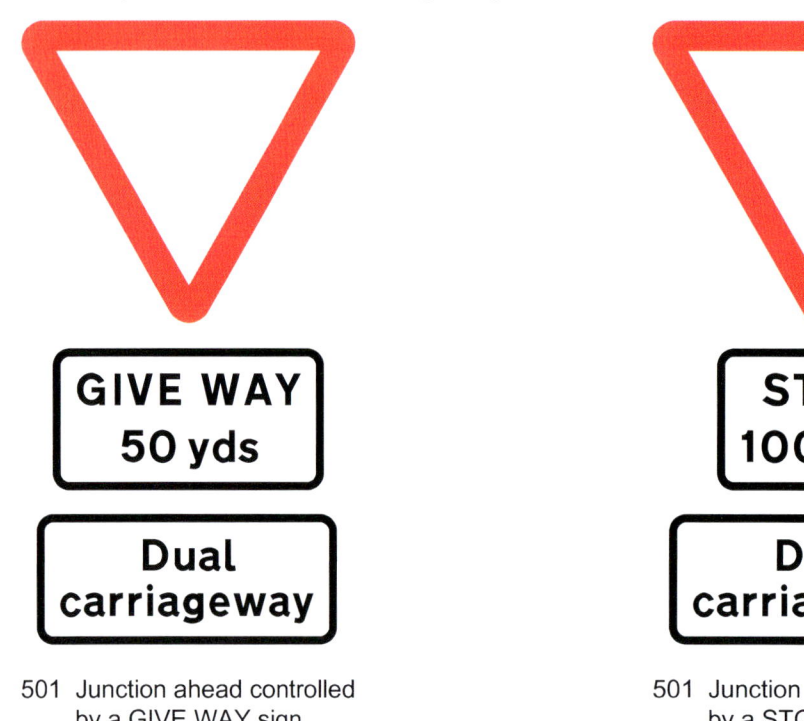

501 Junction ahead controlled by a GIVE WAY sign

501 Junction ahead controlled by a STOP sign

Diagram 501 supplementary plates may not be used alone. The distance plate must always be used and may be varied. The "Dual carriageway" supplementary plate may be omitted.

Figure 2-1 Diagram 501 (S2-6-1) Junction ahead controlled by GIVE WAY / STOP sign

Table 2-1 Advance warning sign criteria, sizes and siting

85th percentile speed (mph)	Clear visibility distance below which an advance warning sign should be provided (m)	Size of advance warning sign (mm)[1]	Supplementary plate x-height (mm)[1]	Distance of advance warning sign from stop or give way line (m)[2,3]
Up to 30	45	600	62.5	45
31 to 40	60	750 (600)	75 (62.5)	45-110
41 to 50	90 (150)	900 (750)	100 (75)	110-180
Over 50	150	1200 (900)	125 (100)	180-245

NOTES

1. Alternative sign sizes are shown in brackets. As these are safety-critical signs warning of a requirement to give way or stop, the smaller alternative should be used only where physical constraints make this necessary or, exceptionally, where special amenity considerations apply. A larger size than

recommended may be used where the accident record justifies greater emphasis, as may the greater clear visibility distance in column 2. The size of the supplementary plate is matched to the corresponding sign, e.g. 62.5 mm with 600 mm, 100 mm with 900 mm.

2. Reference should be made to Note 5 in **Appendix A** for more specific guidance on siting distance.

3. The distance shown on the supplementary plate must always be in yards, to the nearest 10 yards. Metres must not be used.

2.2 Priority junctions

2.2.1. Signs to diagrams 504.1 (S2-2-1, see **Figure 2-2**), 505.1 (S2-2-2, see **Figure 2-3**), 506.1 (S2-2-3, see **Figure 2-4**) and 507.1 (S2-2-4, see **Figure 2-5**) indicate the presence of a junction. The priority route is indicated by the thicker part of the route symbol. This may not necessarily be a route of the same status or with the same route number. The signs may be used only on the priority route, i.e. the width of the part of the symbol indicating the approach arm must not be varied. Diagram 505.1 must not be used on an approach that does not have priority at the junction. Where advance warning of the junction is considered necessary on the non-priority approach, diagram 501 with the appropriate distance plate should be used.

2.2.2. In diagrams 504.1, 506.1 and 507.1 the thicker part of the route symbol indicates the priority route, except that in diagrams 504.1 and 507.1 the thicker symbol must not indicate that a priority route is crossing ahead; the STOP or GIVE WAY sign to diagram 601.1 or 602 (S9-2-1 or S9-2-2) should be used in these circumstances. Details of the variants are shown on the working drawings (see **1.6.1**). No other modifications are permitted.

2.2.3. The sign to diagram 507.1 should be used only in the following circumstances:

a) where the 85th percentile speed of traffic is 30 mph or less and the stagger does not exceed 50 m, or

b) where the 85th percentile speed of traffic is greater than 30 mph and the stagger does not exceed 120 m.

2.2.4. If the priority route is itself the staggered route through the junction, diagram 507.1 must not be used, but a map-type advance direction sign might be beneficial. In all other cases, the two junctions should be signed individually with signs to diagram 506.1. A supplementary distance plate (see section **17**) should be provided at the second sign in cases where the siting distance shown in column 4 of **Table A-1** in **Appendix A** is greater than the distance between the two junctions.

2.2.5. Warning signs should not generally be used where the indication of a junction is given by a map-type advance direction sign. Nor is a warning sign normally required when a stack-type advance direction sign is used, except where the layout will not otherwise be apparent, e.g. at a staggered crossroads. Signs are required at junctions controlled by traffic signals only in certain circumstances (see Chapter 6). Exceptionally, warning signs may be provided in addition to advance direction signs where visibility is so poor that drivers are unable to obtain an adequate advance view of the junction or the directional signs associated with it.

2.2.6. Junction warning signs should be used sparingly where there is a justification. They are not normally provided on very minor rural roads, nor in urban areas where road users can expect to encounter junctions and signing every junction is both impracticable and increases clutter. They may of course be used where a specific need has been identified.

Figure 2-2 Diagram 504.1 (S2-2-1) Crossroads ahead

Figure 2-3 Diagram 505.1 (S2-2-2) T-junction ahead (alternative types)

These signs may be used with diagram 511 or a distance plate

Figure 2-4 Diagram 506.1 (S2-2-3) Side road ahead (Alternative types)

These signs may be used with diagram 511 or a distance plate

Figure 2-5 Diagram 507.1 (S2-2-4) Staggered junction ahead (Alternative types)

2.3 Traffic merge

2.3.1. A sign to diagram 508.1 (S2-2-5, see **Figure 2-6**) or 509.1 (S2-2-6, see **Figure 2-7**) is used to give warning where two physically separated streams of traffic proceeding in the same direction join the same carriageway. These signs may be used only in situations where the traffic stream joining from a slip road crosses a road marking to diagram 1010 and is required to concede priority to any through traffic. They are not intended for use at lane gain junctions where one or more traffic lanes are added to the main carriageway. Diagrams 873 and 874 (S11-2-14) may be used in these circumstances.

Figure 2-6
Diagram 508.1 (S2-2-5)
Traffic merges ahead from the left

Figure 2-7
Diagram 509.1 (S2-2-6)
Traffic merges ahead onto main carriageway

2.3.2. The sign to diagram 508.1 is used to warn that there is traffic joining on the left hand side and should be sited on the left of the main carriageway. The sign to diagram 509.1 is used to warn drivers that they are about to join a main carriageway and may have to concede priority. Neither sign is reversible.

2.3.3. Traffic merge warning signs should normally be used only in the following circumstances:

a) where there is no other advance signing on a main carriageway indicating a junction ahead, e.g. where there is an access slip road, but no exit slip road preceding it to alert drivers to the likelihood of joining traffic, or

b) where there is a series of closely-spaced junctions which are a mixture of lane gain and lane merge (but see **2.3.4**), or

c) where it is not apparent to drivers that they are on a slip road (e.g. a former main road through a village joining a by-pass, or the main carriageway of a motorway joining another motorway).

2.3.4. Rectangular merge signs to diagrams 873 and 874 may be more appropriate in the circumstance described in where there is a series of closely-spaced junctions which are a mixture of lane gain and lane merge (but see Rectangular merge signs to diagrams 873 and 874 may be more appropriate in the circumstance described in where there is a series of closely-spaced junctions which are a mixture of lane gain and lane merge (but see **b)** above.

2.3.5. A distance plate should be used when the distance between the sign and the merge point is different from that recommended in **Appendix A** (but see **1.9.1**).

2.4 Roundabouts

2.4.1. The sign to diagram 510 (S2-2-7, see **Figure 2-8**) should not be used to indicate the approach to a roundabout where adequate warning is conveyed by a map-type advance direction sign or where the roundabout is clearly visible to approaching drivers. It may be used with supplementary plates to diagram 511 (S2-3-1), 513.1A (S2-2-4) or a distance. "Adverse camber" may be used in place of the 513.1A lorry adverse camber plate. The roundabout warning sign should be used only for true roundabouts. It should not be used to give advance warning of a gyratory system or where the approach to an otherwise standard roundabout is controlled by signals.

2.4.2. On high standard all-purpose dual carriageway roads subject to a speed limit of 70 mph, diagram 510 should be used in addition to the map-type advance direction sign and be supplemented by a plate to diagram 511 "REDUCE SPEED NOW" (see **Figure 2-9**). One sign and plate should be situated on the central reservation 500 m in advance of the roundabout, with a duplicate on the left side 450 m in advance (see also **5.2.5** and **5.4.1**). It should be noted that, in addition to diagram 510, diagram 511 may only be used in combination with diagram 504.1, 505.1, 506.1, 507.1, 510, 512, 512.1, 512.2, 512.3, 513, 516, 517, 520, 523.1, 524.1, 528 or 556.

2.4.3. The "REDUCE SPEED NOW" plate may be used with the diagrams detailed, where it is considered that a warning sign alone might not result in a sufficient reduction of speed to enable the hazard to be negotiated in safety.

Figure 2-8
Diagram 510 (S2-2-7) Roundabout ahead

Figure 2-9
Diagram 511 (S2-3-1) Reduce speed now

2.4.4. Where a roundabout on such a road follows a series of grade separated junctions, the signing described in **2.4.2** should be supplemented by an additional sign to diagram 510 on each side of the carriageway, plated with diagram 572 "½ mile". On other roads, where accidents result from excessive approach speeds, signs to diagram 510 should be sited in accordance with the recommendations in **Appendix A**.

2.4.5. Where further emphasis is needed on high-speed approaches on dual carriageway roads, the countdown markers to diagrams 823, 824 and 825 may be used, sited 300, 200 and 100 yards respectively from the give way line. The background colour must be changed to green when used on a primary route, and white (with black symbols and border) on a non-primary route. The signs should normally be mounted in pairs on each side of the carriageway, with the signs on the central reservation being reversed so that the bars incline downwards to the left.

2.4.6. The sign to diagram 7014 (S13-6-37, see **Figure 2-10**) with the legend "NEW ROUNDABOUT AHEAD" (see **1.8.5** for guidance on size) may be erected to warn of a new roundabout. Its use is restricted to a period of not more than 3 months from completion of the works, after which it must be removed. A remove by date must be placed on the back of the sign indicating the three month expiry (S13-7-7 and Schedule 13, Direction 12).

A distance in yards to the nearest 10 yards may be
added before, or substituted for the word "AHEAD"

Figure 2-10 Diagram 7014 (S13-6-37) New roundabout ahead

3 DEVIATION OF ROUTE

3.1 Bend signs

3.1.1. Diagram 512 (S2-2-8, see **Figure 3-1**) may be used to give advance warning of a bend which a driver might find difficult to negotiate without slowing down and the severity of which cannot easily be seen either by day or by night. The symbol should indicate a bend to the left or right as appropriate. The degree of danger at a bend varies mainly with four factors – the speed of approach, the radius of curvature, the superelevation and the skid resistance of the road surface. No uniform objective test can be applied and traffic authorities must rely on a subjective assessment of these factors when deciding whether or not to use the sign. Care should be taken to ensure that a route is signed uniformly.

3.1.2. The radius of curvature not only affects the safe speed appropriate to the bend, it might also reduce forward visibility so that drivers need to slow down.

3.1.3. The sign should be used sparingly and only to indicate a bend hazard. It should not be used simply to allay local apprehension regarding the speed of traffic. Over-use of the sign could compromise its contribution to road safety and add to sign clutter.

3.1.4. On high standard all-purpose dual carriageway roads, consideration should be given to erecting the signs in advance of bends of radius less than 450 metres.

3.1.5. Edge of carriageway markings may be used with this sign. It might also be appropriate to change the centre line to a warning line. Chapter 5 gives further guidance on the use of these markings.

3.1.6. Where junctions which warrant signing in accordance with **2.2.1** occur on sharp bends, use of diagrams 512.1, 512.2 or 512.3 (S2-2-9 to 11, see **Figure 3-2**, **Figure 3-3** & **Figure 3-4**) avoids the need for separate signs. These signs may be used with diagram 511, 513.2, 513.1A, "Adverse camber", "Keep in low gear", "Oncoming vehicles in middle of road" plate or "For" and a distance plate.

3.1.7. The sign to diagram 513 (S2-2-12, see **Figure 3-5**) should be used only where bends of similar severity follow in close proximity. The appropriate symbol must be used to suit the road layout; drivers are likely to be misled if the wrong symbol is used. The sign should be used only when the distance between the bends is less than that given in **Table 3-1**. See **Appendix A** for further guidance on the size and siting of warning signs.

3.1.8. A plate with the legend "For" and a distance (see section **17**) should be used under diagram 513 where a series of bends follow each other at distance intervals less than those referred to in the table. Where a double bend sign is used with a distance plate, bends or combinations of bends occurring within the distance shown on the plate should not be signed individually. However, they may be highlighted individually using diagram 515 (see **3.4.1** to **3.4.6**).

Figure 3-1 Diagram 512 (S2-2-8) Bend ahead

Figure 3-2 Diagram 512.1 (S2-2-9) Junction on the outside of a bend ahead (Alternative types)

Figure 3-3 Diagram 512.2 (S2-2-10) Junction on the inside of a bend ahead (Alternative types)

Figure 3-4 Diagram 512.3 (S2-2-11) Crossroads on a bend ahead (Alternative types)

Figure 3-5 Diagram 513 (S2-2-12) Double bend or series of bends ahead (Alternative types)

Table 3-1 Diagram 513 "Double bend ahead" sign criteria

85th percentile speed (mph)	Sign size (mm)	Maximum distance between bends (m)
Up to 30	600	100
31 to 40	750	200
41 to 50	900	250
51 to 60	1200	300
Over 60	1500	350

NOTE: The distance between bends is measured from the end of one bend to the start of the next.

3.2 Adverse camber

3.2.1. Use of a plate with the legend "Adverse camber" to supplement a bend warning sign may be appropriate for signing a sharp bend where no superelevation has been applied. The sign may be used in other circumstances where loss of control accidents are attributed to insufficient superelevation, e.g. a right hand bend on a steep downhill gradient, or when circulating a roundabout. However, over-use will devalue the sign and it should be used only where the problem is likely to be severe.

3.2.2. Drivers should expect to encounter adverse or insufficient camber on roundabouts. While approach alignment should ideally ensure that vehicles, particularly HGVs, enter the roundabout at a safe speed, this is not always possible. Where there is a problem of large vehicles overturning on the entry to, or circulatory carriageway of, a roundabout, the sign to diagram 513.1A (S2-3-4, see **Figure 3-6**) can be considered. This may be used only in combination with diagram 512, 512.1, 512.2, 512.3 or 513. "Max speed 20" in the lower panel can be omitted. The advisory speed limit may be varied. Although this sign includes a pictorial representation of an overturning lorry, it lacks the recognisable red triangle. It should therefore be used only to supplement standard warning signs.

Road bends to left   Road bends to right

Figure 3-6 Diagram 513.1A (S2-2-4) Risk of lorries overturning on adverse camber and maximum speed advised (Alternative types)

3.3 Maximum speed advised

3.3.1. The advisory speed sign to diagram 513.2 "Maximum speed advised" (S2-3-2, see **Figure 3-7**) is prescribed for use only in combination with the "Loose chippings" sign to diagram 7009 (see Loose chippings arising from surface dressing operations can pose a hazard either due to being thrown up into the path of oncoming vehicles or by causing vehicles to skid on the loose surface. While works are taking place, the sign to diagram 7009 (S13-2-10, see **11.4.1**), the "Other danger ahead" sign to diagram 562 (when used in a temporary situation) or the bend warning signs to diagrams 512, 512.1, 512.2, 512.3 or 513 (see **3.1**). The sign should be used sparingly, as in general it should be for drivers to judge what speed to adopt. It is not easy to determine a standard safe speed to negotiate a bend; factors which influence this include radius of curvature, camber/superelevation, road surface condition and type of vehicle. The sign may be used where the road layout is such that a driver might be misled, e.g. at an exit from a high-speed road where significant slowing is required before negotiating a sharp bend. It may also be used on high-speed roads where the horizontal design radius cannot be achieved, but a lower mandatory speed limit is not imposed on that bend. It must not be used with mandatory speed limit signs, nor in place of repeater signs.

Figure 3-7 Diagram 513.2 (S2-3-2) Maximum speed advised

3.3.2. An alternative to diagram 513.2, where drivers tend to enter a bend at excessive speed, is to plate the bend warning sign with diagram 511 "REDUCE SPEED NOW" (see **2.4.2**).

3.4 Chevron signs

3.4.1. The sign to diagram 515 (see **Figure 3-8**) may be used on roundabouts to face traffic on each approach and elsewhere to denote sharp changes in the direction of a road where a "bend" sign alone would not be a sufficient warning. The sign may also be used at a T-junction where the major road turns through 90°. Care should be taken to ensure that a route is signed uniformly, with successive bends of similar severity treated consistently.

Figure 3-8 Diagram 515 (S2-6-3) Sharp deviation of route

3.4.2. Because the sign is often mounted in a position where it is especially vulnerable to being struck by a vehicle of which the driver has lost control, supports that will yield easily under impact should be considered (see also **3.4.9**).

3.4.3. Chevron signs should never be mounted one immediately above the other, as this produces a confusing zig-zag pattern. They must not be supplemented by diagonal stripes, chequering or other unlawful background markings. Where greater conspicuity is required, perhaps because of the background the sign is viewed against, a yellow backing board may be used. The width of the yellow area should not be less than half the horizontal width of the white chevron. Alternatively, a larger size sign to diagram 515 may be provided. Increasing the size of the chevrons will result in the sign being seen earlier, provided that sufficient sight distance is available. The improved conspicuity and legibility distance might encourage a greater speed reduction.

3.4.4. The sign is prescribed in heights of 400 mm, 600 mm and 800 mm. The smallest size is intended to be used where the 85th percentile speed on the approach to the bend does not exceed 50 mph. The 600 mm size should be used for approach speeds between 51 and 60 mph, and 800 mm where speeds exceed 60 mph. To minimise the potential danger of sharp edges, the corners may be rounded, with a radius not greater than 10 mm. When sited adjacent to areas used by pedestrians, the vertical edges of the sign plates should also be protected, e.g. by the use of rectangular posts flush with the edges of the sign.

3.4.5. The number and direction of the chevrons may be varied. However, a sign should normally comprise a minimum of two chevrons. A series of single chevrons is difficult to install and maintain in alignment and should be used only where there is inadequate space for longer assemblies. On long bends, a greater number of chevrons may be required. Single chevrons are also vulnerable to being turned. This is potentially serious as they might then give a misleading impression to a driver approaching from the opposite direction. This can be avoided by using two posts, or one square post. The shortest prescribed sign is a single module extending from the tip of one chevron to the tip of the next.

3.4.6. Care must be taken when positioning chevrons to ensure that they do not mislead drivers from the opposite direction. Chevrons signs should be placed so that vehicles are required to pass in front of them and not behind. They should never be used in advance of a bend as an alternative to diagram 512.

3.4.7. The normal mounting height is 1000 mm to the lower edge of the sign, but greater mounting heights may be appropriate to meet particular circumstances, e.g. where a bend is partly hidden over the brow of a hill. When used on the central island of a roundabout, the height should be measured from the kerb level to the centre of the chevron, and the sign may be accompanied by the directional arrow to diagram 606 (see Chapter 3). This should be mounted at the same level but in front of the chevrons to reduce clutter, but may be positioned above. At least one complete chevron should be visible on each side.

3.4.8. These signs may be used on all roundabouts other than mini-roundabouts. In practice it will not be necessary to use them at the very smallest roundabouts, provided the speed limit is 30 mph or less, the diagram 606 arrow being sufficient. They should normally be used whenever the diameter of the central island exceeds 8 metres.

3.4.9. If the sign is used in the central reserve or on the off side of a slip road on the immediate approach to a roundabout, it should not be sited where it would impair the driver's view of circulating traffic.

3.4.10. Diagram 515 may also be made from flexible material and designed to recover when struck by a vehicle. A yellow border may be added to the outside edge of the part that forms the chevrons. It may include a direction arrow to diagram 606, formed as part of the flexible elements, placed over the chevrons and any yellow border. Its use at particularly vulnerable locations might help to reduce maintenance costs.

4.1 General

4.1.1. Signs to diagrams 516 (S2-2-13, see **Figure 4-1**) or 517 (S2-2-14, see **Figure 4-2**) should be used where a reduction in width on a single carriageway road presents a hazard. Dual carriageway situations are dealt with in **4.1.6**. Signs will not normally be needed if the narrowing does not result in the loss of a lane and involves a taper no more severe than indicated in **Table 4-1**. However, signs should be provided regardless of the rate of taper where a lane is lost on a single carriageway road or where the reduction in width is so great that the centre line marking has to be omitted (see also **4.1.4**). The "REDUCE SPEED NOW" plate (see **Figure 2-9** & **2.4.2**) should be used if a significant speed reduction is advisable. These signs must not be used to warn of the termination of a dual carriageway (see **5.1**).

Figure 4-1 Diagram 516 (S2-2-13)
Road narrows on both sides ahead

Figure 4-2 Diagram 517 (S2-2-14)
Road narrows on one side ahead
(Alternative types)

Table 4-1 Taper criteria for warning sign

85th percentile speed (mph)	Taper
Up to 30	1 in 40
31 to 40	1 in 60
41 to 50	1 in 80
Over 50	1 in 100

4.1.2. The signs may be supplemented by edge lines, hatched markings and hazard markers to diagram 560. A supplementary plate "Oncoming vehicles in middle of road" may be used if drivers are likely to be surprised by an oncoming vehicle (see **18.2.1**).

4.1.3. The sign to diagram 517 should be used in preference to 516 if the narrowing occurs mainly on one side of the road. At the termination of a single carriageway climbing lane, the alignment should place the onus on the overtaking driver to rejoin the nearside lane and the sign to diagram 872.1 is used in advance of the start of the loss of the right hand lane at the distance specified in **Table 4-2**, and repeated at half this distance. The second sign is not necessary if the 85th percentile speed is below 50 mph. Details of road marking layouts and tapers for climbing lanes can be found in Chapter 5 and TD 9 in Volume 6 of DMRB.

4.1.4. Where a road with two lanes in one direction, other than a climbing lane, narrows to a single lane, or a road with a single lane in each direction narrows to a single track, an advance warning sign with the appropriate supplementary plate with the legend "Single file traffic" (see **Figure 4-3**) or "Single track road" (see **Figure 4-4**) should always be provided. If the sign has to be sited at a distance from the hazard significantly different from that recommended in

Appendix A, a distance may be added in accordance with S18-3. An indication of the distance over which the restriction extends may be given, e.g. "Single file traffic for 400 yds". If the road indicated is a side road, an arrow may be added, pointing horizontally to the left or to the right. Details are shown on the working drawings.

Single file traffic	**Single track road**
May be used only in combination with diagram 516, 517 or 520	May be used only in combination with diagram 516 or 517
Figure 4-3 Single file traffic in each direction	**Figure 4-4** Road wide enough for one line of vehicles only

4.1.5. If a road is wide enough for only one line of vehicles but there are passing places marked with diagram 822 "PASSING PLACE" (S11-2-9, see **Figure 4-5**), diagram 821 "Single track road with passing places" (S11-2-8, see **Figure 4-6**) should be used at each end of the single track section. The legend "with passing places" may be varied to "No passing places for" and a distance in yards or miles or "Use passing places to permit overtaking".

4.1.6. The loss of a lane on a dual carriageway road, on a slip road at a grade separated junction or on a one-way street should be indicated using the sign to diagram 872.1 (S11-2-15, see **Figure 4-7**). The sign illustrated is for use on a motorway. The background colour is varied to dark green when the sign is used on a primary route and to white with black symbols and border when used on a non-primary route. The number of ahead arrows and the distance may be varied. The lower panel may be omitted.

4.1.7. The size of diagram 872.1 is determined by the measurement across the arrowhead. A sign should be placed on each side of the carriageway, and the pair repeated on roads with higher traffic speeds. Sizes and distances from the start of the taper are detailed in **Table 4-2**. On motorways and other dual three-lane carriageway roads subject to a 70 mph speed limit, three pairs of signs should normally be provided, at 800, 360 and 180 metres from the start of the taper.

4.1.8. Guidance on the associated road markings where the number of lanes is reduced on a high-speed road can be found in Chapter 5.

PASSING PLACE

Figure 4-5 Diagram 822 (S11-2-9) Passing place on a narrow road

Single track road with passing places

Single track road No passing places for ½ mile

Single track road Use passing places to permit overtaking

Figure 4-6 Diagram 821 (S11-2-8) Road ahead wide enough for one line of vehicles, and providing information about passing places

200 yards

200 yards

Figure 4-7 Diagram 872.1 (S11-2-15) Reduction in the number of traffic lanes ahead (Alternative types)

Table 4-2 Size and siting of signs to diagram 872.1

85th percentile speed (mph)	Size of arrowhead (mm)	x-height of legend (mm)	First signs on approach		Second signs on approach	
			Distance to start of taper (m)	Legend	Distance to start of taper (m)	Legend
Up to 30	240	120	45[1]	None	None	None
31 to 40	240	120	135	150 yds	None	None
41 to 50	320	160	180	200 yds	None	None
51 to 60	320	160	270	300 yds	135	150 yds
Over 60	400	200	360	400 yds	180	200 yds
Motorway[2]	400 (480)[3]	200 (240)[3]	800	½ mile	360[4]	400 yds

NOTES

1. On two-lane carriageways subject to a 30 mph speed limit, a single sign mounted on the side of the road on which the lane is to be lost may be adequate, although the possibility of obscuration by parked vehicles should be considered.

2. Also all-purpose dual three-lane carriageway roads subject to a 70 mph speed limit.

3. Bracketed dimension is used where there are four or more lanes.

4. A third pair of signs should be provided at a distance of 180 m indicating a distance of 200 yds.

5.1 Two-way traffic

5.1.1. The signs to diagrams 520 (S2-2-15, see **Figure 5-1**) and 521 (S2-2-16, see **Figure 5-2**) indicate the resumption of two-way traffic on a single carriageway road after a length of dual carriageway and, in the case of diagram 521, after a one-way road. The sign to diagram 522 indicates a two-way road crossing ahead (S2-2-17, see **Figure 5-3** and **5.2.2**).

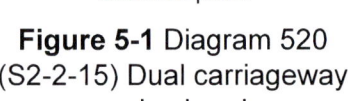

May be used with diagram 511, a distance, "Single file traffic" with or without a distance or "Single file traffic for" and a distance plate

Figure 5-1 Diagram 520 (S2-2-15) Dual carriageway ends ahead

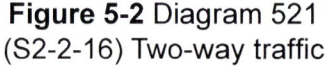

May be used with "For" and a distance or a distance plate

Figure 5-2 Diagram 521 (S2-2-16) Two-way traffic

Figure 5-3 Diagram 522 (S2-2-17) Two-way traffic on route crossing ahead

5.1.2. Road markings consisting of pairs of opposing arrows to diagram 1038, indicating the ahead direction, may be used to supplement the sign to diagram 521. This may be particularly helpful where a single carriageway road is similar in appearance to one carriageway of a dual carriageway road.

5.2 End of one-way road

5.2.1. Diagram 521 (see **Figure 5-2**) should be used to indicate a change from one to two-way traffic, and also at the commencement of any two-way side roads that form a junction with a one-way road. It should be erected as close as possible to the beginning of two-way working, consistent with being readily visible to turning traffic, and may be repeated after 100 metres.

5.2.2. Diagram 522 (S2-2-17, see **Figure 5-3**) is generally used on a one-way road to indicate that a road it joins or one that crosses it carries two-way traffic. It is normally sited on the back of the "no entry" sign. However, it might also be helpful on a two-way road where it is crossed by another two-way road after a succession of intersections with one-way roads. It is not normally appropriate in an urban low speed environment where one way roads are regularly encountered and other visual clues exist as to the nature of the road. It may be used with a distance plate.

End of dual carriageway

5.2.3. The road markings required where a dual carriageway road reduces to a single carriageway are detailed in Chapter 5. **Table 5-1** lists the appropriate tapers. The sign to diagram 520 should be sited in advance of the end of the dual carriageway at the usual distance appropriate to warning signs (see **Appendix A**). The sign to diagram 521 (see **Figure 5-2**) should be erected at or as near as possible to the beginning of two-way working, and may be repeated after 100 metres.

5.2.4. Where traffic speeds are high, as on inter-urban roads, more comprehensive signing as shown in **Figure 5-4** should be provided.

Table 5-1 Taper at end of dual carriageway

85th percentile speed (mph)	Taper
Up to 40	1 in 40
41 to 50	1 in 45
51 to 60	1 in 50
Over 60	1 in 55

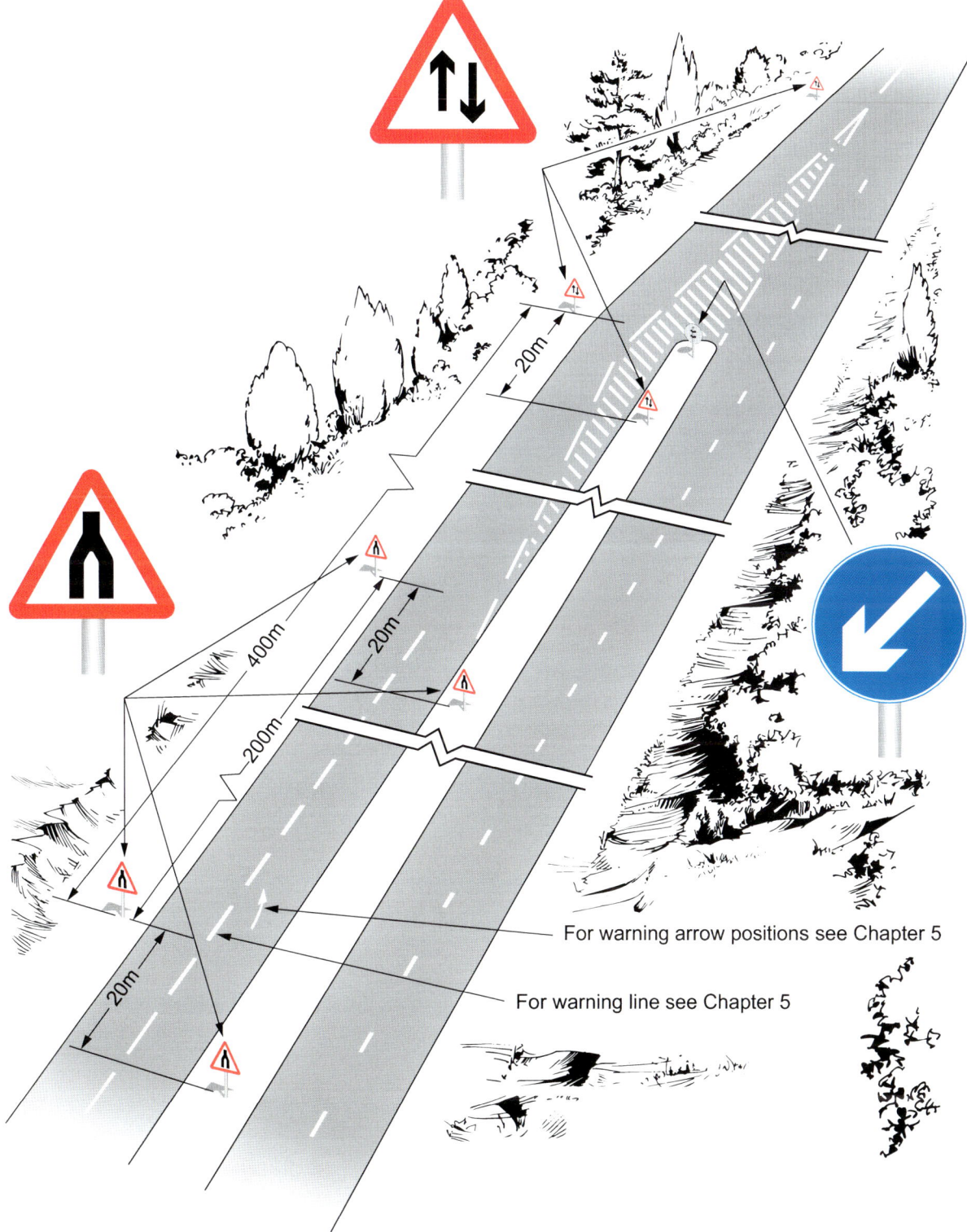

For warning arrow positions see Chapter 5

For warning line see Chapter 5

Figure 5-4 Signing at the end of a rural dual carriageway road

5.2.5. Where a high-speed dual carriageway road ends at a roundabout, signs to diagram 520 should be erected on both sides of the carriageway approximately 100 metres before the roundabout. A sign to diagram 521 should be erected approximately 50 metres after the roundabout. Warning signs to diagram 510 should also be used as appropriate (see **2.4.1** to **2.4.4**).

5.2.6. Where speeds on the dual carriageway road are high, but the length of dualling is so short that it would not be possible to site the signs in accordance with **Figure 5-1**, they may be sited at not less than one half the normal distance from the end of the central reservation. Duplicating the sign on the right hand side of the carriageway is recommended.

5.3 Start of dual carriageway

5.3.1. On a single carriageway road which widens to a dual carriageway for a length of at least 400 metres, an advance sign to diagram 818.1 "Dual carriageway ahead" (S11-2-11, see **Figure 5-5**) should be provided. Siting distances, normally measured back from the nose of the central hatch marking at the start of the dual carriageway, are similar to those indicated in **Appendix A** for warning triangles. If the dual carriageway is shorter than 400 metres, no advance sign should be provided. The sign to diagram 818.1A (S11-2-12, see **Figure 5-6**) may be used to warn drivers that a dualled length is short and so might not be long enough to permit overtaking. The sign may display distances of "¼ mile" or "½ mile" only.

Figure 5-5 Diagram 818.1 (S11-2-11)   **Figure 5-6** Diagram 818.1A (S11-2-12)
Section of dual carriageway ahead   Distance over which a short length of dual
(distance may be reduced or omitted)   carriageway road beginning directly ahead extends

5.3.2. Further advance warning up to a distance of two miles may also be given by a sign to diagram 818.1. This sign may be used to encourage drivers to delay overtaking until the dual carriageway is reached. Distances greater than two miles are not permitted, as this might result in impatient drivers trying to overtake on an unsuitable length of road.

5.3.3. For guidance on the appropriate x-height for these signs, see **Table 5-2**.

Table 5-2 Size of dual carriageway signs

85th percentile speed (mph)	x-height (see note) (mm)
Up to 30	75
31 to 40	100
41 to 50	125
Over 50	150 (200)

NOTE: The larger size shown in brackets may be used on high standard single carriageway roads where speeds are high (e.g. on 10 m wide carriageways).

5.3.4. "Keep left" signs (diagram 610, S3-2-3, see Chapter 3) should always be placed at the start of the central reservation, and at any gaps.

5.4 Roundabouts on dual carriageways

5.4.1. A plain bollard may be used on the central reservation of a dual carriageway or on the splitter island of any other road leaving a roundabout. A bollard may be dispensed with where an internally or externally lit direction sign is provided in such a position. Further guidance on the signing of roundabouts may be found in **2.4.1** to **2.4.6**, **3.4.1**, **3.4.6** to **3.4.9** and **5.2.5**.

5.5 Gap closures

5.5.1. Where a gap in the central reservation of a dual carriageway has been closed, a temporary sign to diagram 7014 (see **1.8.5** for guidance on size) varied to "GAP CLOSED AHEAD" (S13-6-37, see **Figure 5-7**) should be provided, warning drivers of the changed layout. This should be sited on the central reservation a suitable distance in advance of the closure. It will usually be helpful to add the distance in yards (to the nearest 10 yards) on a separate line after "CLOSED", "AHEAD" may then be omitted. This sign must display a remove by date on the reverse, limited to a maximum period of three months after completion of the works (S13-7-8 and S13-12, Direction 12). A "no right turn" sign (diagram 612) may be placed on the central reservation immediately preceding the former gap. This should be removed at the same time as the GAP CLOSED sign. Junction warning signs may need to be removed or replaced (e.g. diagram 506.1 indicating a side road might have to be substituted for diagram 504.1 indicating a crossroads). Amended side road signing should be in accordance with **5.6.1**.

Figure 5-7 Diagram 7014 (S13-6-37)
Gap closed ahead (variant)

5.6 Side roads

5.6.1. Where a minor road crosses or joins a dual carriageway, GIVE WAY or STOP signs (see Chapter 3) should normally be provided on the minor road, supplemented by a "Dual carriageway" plate to diagram 608 (see **2.1.1**). Where advance warning is needed, signs to diagram 501 with the STOP or GIVE WAY plate as appropriate should be erected in accordance with **Table 2-1**. The "Dual carriageway" plate may be provided below these signs also.

5.6.2. Special care is needed in signing minor road junctions with dual carriageway roads if the carriageways are separated by a very wide central reservation and the further carriageway could be mistaken for a separate road or cannot easily be seen by a driver on the minor road. In such cases, as an additional safeguard, NO ENTRY (diagram 1046) should be marked on the nearer carriageway to prevent drivers from turning right into it. It may also be appropriate to erect "no entry" signs (diagram 616) on each side of the nearer carriageway, angled so as to be seen by a driver attempting a right turn. The no entry sign must only be placed to indicate the effect of a traffic regulation order. If the layout is not self-evident, a map-type sign on the minor road approach might be helpful.

5.6.3. On a side road which joins a dual carriageway road where there is no gap in the central reservation, a "turn left ahead" sign (diagram 609) together with an associated "Dual carriageway" plate should be used. A "turn left" sign (diagram 606, see Chapter 3) with a "Dual carriageway" plate should be erected on the central reservation opposite the side road.

6.1 General

6.1.1. Steep hills are signed using diagrams 523.1 (S2-2-18, see **Figure 6-1**) and 524.1 (S2-2-19, see **Figure 6-2**) together with associated plates. The gradient is calculated using the tangent of the angle concerned, although in practice it makes little difference whether the sine or the tangent is used. The gradient on signs must be expressed as a percentage; old signs showing a ratio may remain in place until life-expired.

6.1.2. The sign to diagram 523.1 should normally be used only where the gradient is 10% or more. The actual gradient to the nearest whole number should be indicated on the sign, e.g. a gradient of 10.4% should be signed as 10%, but 10.6% as 11%.

Figure 6-1 Diagram 523.1 (S2-2-18)
Steep hill downwards ahead

Figure 6-2 Diagram 524.1 (S2-2-19)
Steep hill upwards ahead

6.1.3. On very steep or long hills where additional warning is considered necessary, the sign may be repeated as appropriate, supplemented with the "Low gear now", "Keep in low gear" or "Low gear for" plate (see **Figure 6-3**) and a distance plate with or without a left or right arrow. These plates must not be used alone. The sign may also be used with diagram 511 (see **2.4.3**).

6.1.4. The circumstances justifying the additional plates cannot be stated precisely. Traffic authorities, after consulting the police, will have to assess the need to advise drivers to engage a lower gear and gauge the likelihood of this instruction being respected. It is difficult to persuade drivers to select a lower gear to descend a long hill if their own assessment of the need is different. Where drivers have a good view of the descent and can make their own judgement, then an instruction to change gear will be obeyed only if they think it correct. Instructions should not be given if they are likely to be ignored and any existing signs which are not being respected should be removed.

Low gear now	**Keep in low gear**	**Low gear for 1½ miles**
May be used only in combination with diagram 523.1 or 524.1	May be used only in combination with diagram 512, 512.1, 512.2, 512.3, 513, 523.1, 524.1 or 554.1	May be used only in combination with diagram 523.1 or 524.1. The distance may be varied.

Figure 6-3 "Low gear" supplementary plates (Alternative types)

6.1.5. "Low gear" plates are not normally used unless the gradient overall or in part exceeds 12% and the hill is longer than 800 metres. They are more likely to be justified where there are also sharp bends.

6.1.6. The instruction to "Keep in low gear" should be used at intervals of not less than 800 metres where the gradient exceeds 12%; it may be accompanied by diagram 554.1 "Try your brakes" (see **10.1.2**). When used in advance of an escape lane, diagram 523.1 should be replaced by 554.1 as shown in **Table 6-1**. Exceptionally, "Keep in low gear" with an accompanying sign may be used at a shorter interval, e.g. where an increase of gradient is hidden from view.

6.1.7. "Steep hill" signs without plates may be repeated on a hill where the gradient steepens but should not be placed at intervals of less than 550 metres unless the gradient increases by 5% or more. On long descents, certain sections may be steep whilst others are below the 10% criterion for provision of signs. It might then be better to treat the steeper parts as separate hills and sign accordingly.

6.1.8. Where an escape lane or arrester bed is available, the "Escape lane ahead" sign to diagram 817.2 (S2-3-3, see **Figure 6-4**) should be used. It should form part of a sequence of signs with "ahead" varied as in **Table 6-1**. The sign may also be varied to show the escape lane to the left on a straight road. Permitted variants are illustrated on the working drawings. The order of the sign plates, from the top, should be: warning sign (523.1 or 554.1): supplementary plate (525 or 526): diagram 817.2.

Table 6-1 Locations of signs for an escape lane

Location	Warning sign	Plate	Variant of 817.2
At top of hill	523.1	525	ahead
400 yards from escape lane	554.1	526	400 yds
200 yards from escape lane	523.1	526	200 yds
At entry to escape lane	523.1	526	arrow

6.1.9. The sign shown in diagram 524.1 should be used only:

a) where the gradient is 15% or more, or

b) where the ascent is longer than 1600 metres and the gradient is 10% or more, in which case the sign should be accompanied by a distance plate (see section **17**).

6.1.10. The supplementary plates "Low gear now", "Keep in low gear" and "Low gear for" and a distance should not normally be used with the ascent warning, except in rare circumstances e.g. where a very sharp increase in gradient is hidden from view and there is a record of accidents due to vehicles stalling and rolling back out of control.

6.1.11. For the sign to diagram 583 and its associated plate (indicating slow-moving vehicles) see **19.2**.

May be used only in combination with diagram 523.1 together with either "Low gear now" or "Keep in low gear", or diagram 554.1 with 526. The word "ahead" may be varied to a distance or an arrow pointing to the left or to the right, or omitted. The angle of the route symbol may be varied to accord with the layout

Figure 6-4 Diagram 817.2 (S2-3-3) Escape lane ahead

7.1 Humped bridges

7.1.1. The sign to diagram 528 (S2-2-20, see **Figure 7-1**) should be used where a hump bridge is so severe that unless drivers are forewarned they might lose control of their vehicles. If visibility is inadequate, double white lines or a hazard line should be laid in accordance with the normal criteria. If the hump bridge hides a further hazard, another sign indicating this should be provided on the same post (with the sign indicating the first hazard encountered placed uppermost). If there is a risk of long vehicles grounding on the bridge, diagram 782 (see **20.4.1**) should be used also, mounted below diagram 528. They should be sited, with a distance plate, on the approach to a junction at which vehicles can divert, and repeated at the standard siting distance from the structure (see **Appendix A**).

7.1.2. Signs to diagram 528.1 (S2-4-1, see **Figure 7-2**) should be used where a bridge parapet, abutment or other obstruction is immediately adjacent to, or encroaches onto, the carriageway. This includes any parapet or abutment on the off side where it would be a hazard to drivers overtaking or passing a temporary obstruction on the near side. In addition to the risk to passing road traffic, damage to a parapet can also result in considerable danger to rail traffic. It is therefore particularly important that signs to diagram 528.1 on parapets or abutments of bridges are correctly installed and maintained to a high standard. The use of these signs helps to make the vulnerable parts of a structure more conspicuous. If the obstruction is accompanied by a narrowing of the carriageway, "road narrows" signs to diagram 516 or 517 (see section **4**) and edge lines should also be used. The signs should be used as in the diagram, sloping downwards towards the carriageway. The Regulations permit the use of yellow material which is both retroreflective and fluorescent (see **7.3.1**).

7.1.3. The sign to diagram 529 (S2-2-21, see **Figure 7-3**) should be used in advance of opening bridges (lifting or swing. If movement onto a bridge is controlled by wig-wag signals to diagram 3014 (S14-2-5, see Chapter 6), a plate to diagram 773 (see **20.1.4**) should be added.

May be used with diagram 511, a distance with or without an arrow pointing to the left or to the right, an arrow pointing to the left or to the right alone, "Oncoming vehicles in middle of road" or 782

Figure 7-1 Diagram 528 (S2-2-20)
Hump bridge ahead

Figure 7-2 Diagram 528.1 (S2-4-1)
End of bridge parapet, abutment wall, tunnel mouth or other obstruction adjacent to the carriageway

May be used with a distance with or without an arrow pointing to the
left or right, an arrow pointing to the left or right alone or diagram 773

Figure 7-3 Diagram 529 (S2-2-21) Opening or swing bridge ahead

7.2 Tunnels

7.2.1. The sign shown in diagram 529.1 (S2-2-22, see **Figure 7-4**) is for use in advance of tunnels, a supplementary plate indicates the distance ahead to the tunnel. If the tunnel is controlled by wig-wag signals, the sign should be supplemented by a plate to diagram 773 (S14-2-6, see **Figure 20-4**).

May be used with a distance with or without an arrow pointing to the
left or right, an arrow pointing to the left or right alone or diagram 773

Figure 7-4 Diagram 529.1 (S2-2-22) Tunnel ahead

7.2.2. The Road Tunnel Safety Regulations 2007 require that a tunnel's length should be indicated on a sign at the portal. This should be done using the sign shown in diagram 892 (S11-2-10, see **Figure 7-5**) or 893 (S11-2-10, see **Figure 7-6**).

Figure 7-5 Diagram 892 (S11-2-10)
Name and length of tunnel on a motorway

Figure 7-6 Diagram 893 (S11-2-10)
Name and length of tunnel on an all-purpose road

7.3 Low bridges

7.3.1. Incidents where road vehicles strike low bridges present a serious hazard to both rail and road users. There is a significant number of reported bridge strikes each year. It takes only a relatively small amount of force to displace bridge girders sufficiently to derail a train. Serious damage can also be caused to arch bridges. It is therefore particularly important that the signs and markings on low bridges are correctly installed and maintained to a high standard. The use of black and yellow hazard markings to diagram 530.2 (S2-5-4, see **Figure 7-12**) or 532.4 (S2-5-3, see **Figure 7-16** and **Figure 7-18**) helps to make the vulnerable parts of a structure more conspicuous. The yellow parts of these markings may be reflectorised, making them much brighter at night; and if retroreflective, may also be fluorescent. The latter greatly increases conspicuity in dull weather and at dusk (see **1.12.2** for further guidance on fluorescence). However, fluorescence is visually intrusive and is therefore best confined to structures that are known to be at risk.

7.3.2. The standard minimum clearance over every part of the carriageway of a public road is 16'-6" (5.03 m). Where the clearance over any part is less than this, signs should be provided. Where a dual carriageway road has hard shoulders with restricted headroom, this should be separately signed, supplemented with the hazard markings in diagram 530.2 or the chord markings used at arch bridges (see **7.8.3** and **7.8.4**).

7.3.3. All bridges and other structures with a headroom of less than 16'-6" (5.03 m) should be clearly signed. The Regulations require heights on new signs to be shown in both imperial and metric units. Imperial and metric heights should be calculated separately (see **7.4** & **7.5**).

7.3.4. The bridge height should be re-measured when works on the road or to the bridge might have affected the available headroom. Permanent signs should be changed if necessary and a temporary sign to diagram 7014.1 (S13-6-39, see **Figure 7-7**), with the height varied as appropriate and a remove by date on the back, may be erected for a period of 6 months following completion of the works.

Figure 7-7 Diagram 7014.1 (S13-6-39) Reduction in bridge headroom ahead

7.3.5. Care should be taken to ensure that vehicles of the maximum length permitted by the Construction and Use Regulations will be able to pass safely under the bridge. This is particularly important where the road dips or hogs sharply or is on a curving alignment under the bridge. Changes in gradient might affect the headroom, e.g. the effective clearance will be reduced for a long wheel base vehicle spanning a dip. Where the road passing under a structure is on a sag curve, the headroom should be measured along the carriageway over a 25 m chord.

7.4 Imperial height

7.4.1. The imperial figure shown on signs to indicate the available headroom should be at least 3 inches less than the measured height to allow a safety margin. If the resulting figure is not a multiple of 3 inches, it should be rounded down to the nearest lower multiple of 3 inches.

>Example 1: measured height 15'-2":
>>**Step 1** subtract 3" to create a safety margin 14'-11"
>>**Step 2** round down to nearest multiple of 3"
>>**Step 3** sign as 14'-9".
>Example 2: measured height 14'-6":
>>**Step 1** subtract 3" to create a safety margin 14'-3"
>>**Step 2** sign as 14'-3" (rounding down not required as already a multiple of 3")

Thus, the maximum headroom that will normally appear on a sign is 16'-0".

7.5 Metric height

7.5.1. To obtain the metric figure shown on signs, the bridge height should be measured to two decimal places, rounding down to the nearest 0.01 m. The following method is then used to calculate the appropriate signed height:

a) if the second decimal digit is 8 or 9, delete it and sign the bridge with the remaining whole number and the first decimal digit;

b) Example 1: measured height 4.19 m:

c) Step 1 remove the final 9 (subtract 0.09 m)

d) Step 2 sign as 4.1 m

e) if the second decimal digit is 7 or less, delete it and reduce the first decimal digit by 1. Sign the bridge with the remaining whole number and first decimal digit, as reduced;

f) Example 2: measured height 4.17 m

g) Step 1 remove the final 7 (subtract 0.07 m)

h) Step 2 reduce first decimal digit by 1 (subtract 0.1 m)

i) Step 3 sign as 4.0 m

7.5.2. The height shown on the sign must be to only one decimal place. The maximum headroom that will normally appear on a sign is 4.9 m.

7.6 Diversion signing

7.6.1. In order to reduce the risk of the driver of an overheight vehicle being confronted with an impassable bridge, it is important that properly planned diversion route signing is provided, certainly where a structure has a history of repeated strikes. In such a case, it is not sufficient to rely on warning signs alone. Diversion route signing may be incorporated into standard junction advance direction signs and flag-type signs, or separately mounted signs to diagrams 818.4 (S12-28-22, see **7.6.3** and **Figure 7-8**) and 818.5 (S12-28-23, see **7.6.4** and **Figure 7-9**) may be provided, or both types of signing may be used together. The sign to diagram 818.4, varied to omit the alternative route, is used to give advance warning of a non-arch bridge. This sign might be appropriate in advance of any diversion route signing or on the immediate approach to a bridge (see **7.7.2**).

7.6.2. The Regulations prescribe both map-type and stack-type advance direction signs for indicating alternative routes avoiding a low bridge. Prohibitory roundels are used where the restriction is mandatory (see **7.7.1**), otherwise the triangular warning signs are used. The flag-type signs at the junction should also incorporate a warning sign or prohibitory sign as appropriate. Directional signs with a prohibitory roundel must also include a distance plate unless the restriction commences at the junction. For design details, see Chapter 7.

7.6.3. An alternative route avoiding a mandatory height restriction may be signed using a variant of the sign to diagram 818.4 (see **Figure 7-10**), at the x-height indicated in **Appendix A**. The sign should be placed where the driver can see it in good time to make the necessary manoeuvre, before the advance direction sign for the next junction at which the routes advised are signed. It is essential that full route continuity signing is provided to the point where the original route is resumed.

7.6.4. At arch bridges, where the available headroom is indicated by a sign to diagram 530A (S2-4-2, see **Figure 7-19**), an alternative route may be signed using a sign to diagram 818.5, at the x-height indicated in **Appendix A**. As with mandatory height restrictions, the sign should be placed where the driver can see it in good time to make the necessary manoeuvre and full route continuity signing should be provided.

"Low bridge" may be varied to "Height limit" or omitted (with the remaining legend placed below the roundel). An arrow pointing horizontally to the left or right may be added or substituted for the distance (with "ahead" omitted in each case). The distance may be varied.

Figure 7-8 Diagram 818.4 (S12-28-22) Nature and location of a prohibition, restriction or requirement with indication of alternative route (variant showing mandatory height limit at low bridge ahead)

An arrow pointing horizontally to the left or right may be added above the diagram 530A symbol. The location may be varied as appropriate or changed to a distance. "ahead" may be added after the distance when no arrow is shown. The alternative route may be omitted or varied as appropriate and may include a reference to a motorway junction. A diversion route symbol may be added.

Figure 7-9 Diagram 818.5 (S12-28-23) Available headroom at low bridge ahead and indication of alternative route (Advance sign for an arch bridge)

An arrow pointing horizontally to the left or right may be added above the roundel. "Low bridge" may be varied to "Height limit" or omitted, with the location varied as appropriate or changed to a distance. "ahead" may be added after the distance when no arrow is shown. The alternative route may be omitted or varied as appropriate and may include a reference to a motorway junction. A diversion route symbol may be added. Details of the permitted variants are shown in S12-28-22.

Figure 7-10 Diagram 818.4 (S12-28-22) Varied to mandatory height limit at low bridge ahead and indication of alternative routes

7.7 Non-arch bridges

7.7.1. Mandatory signs should normally be used at non-arch bridges, as they can give more effective protection than warning signs. Traffic regulation orders are not required for mandatory height limit signs at a bridge, tunnel or similar structure over the highway, but are required for limits imposed for environmental reasons.

7.7.2. The sign to diagram 629.2A (S2-4-5, see **Figure 7-11**) should be mounted on the bridge, as a driver seeing a bridge with no height limit indicated might well assume the headroom to be at least 16'-6". It may also be placed at the roadside in advance of the bridge (in most cases a sign being required on each side of the road), but as it is an offence for drivers of overheight vehicles to pass these signs, they should not be placed where they would prevent legitimately-required access to premises or side roads. Even when diversion signing has been provided, it is still necessary to give proper advance warning of the height restriction. Signs to diagram 530A are not appropriate, as they give no indication of the prohibition. Diagram 818.4, with or without a diversion route should be used; it will sometimes be possible to indicate an escape route for drivers who have missed the diversion signs by siting this sign in advance of the last diversion or turning point before the bridge. If it is much further from the bridge than the usual warning distance indicated in **Appendix A**, another sign to diagram 818.4 may be required at the appropriate place. Diagram 818.4 may also be used to indicate a restriction in a side road by including an arrow on the sign (the legend "ahead" must not be used with the arrow).

This sign may be used with diagram 530.2. The height may be varied.

Figure 7-11 Diagram 629.2A (S2-4-5) Mandatory height restriction (metric and imperial units)

7.7.3. It is not recommended practice to place a warning sign to diagram 530A on a non-arch bridge as an alternative to a mandatory sign, to diagram 629.2A.

7.7.4. The conspicuity of the bridge can be significantly enhanced by use of the marking to diagram 530.2 (S2-5-4, see **Figure 7-12**). Where the yellow parts of the marking are made of retroreflective material, they may also be fluorescent (see **7.3.1**). The first of the two alternative types, with a cut-out for the signs, should normally be used on the lowest part of the bridge elevation. If the construction of the bridge is such that signs cannot be located in this position, the second alternative should be used, with the signs mounted above.

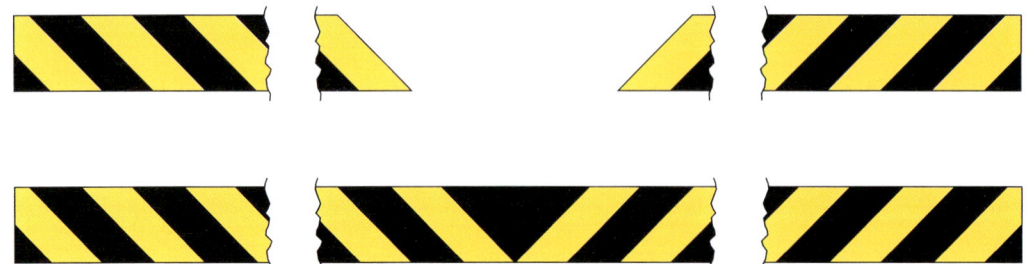

May be used only in combination with diagram 530A or 629.2A

Figure 7-12 Diagram 530.2 (S2-5-4) Reduced headroom at a hazard

7.7.5. The signing on the approach to a non-arch bridge is shown in **Figure 7-13** below.

End of diversion route for overheight vehicles

NOTE: Black and yellow markings on bridge should not extend over verge or footway

Signing at structure

Diagram 629.2A plus conspicuity markings to diagram 530.2

Prohibitory signs, if appropriate (see 7.7.2)

Diagram 629.2A
Note: If access is required to premises, these signs may be replaced by a single sign to diagram 818.4

Advisory sign in advance of last turning opportunity, if needed

Diagram 818.4

Advisory signing in advance of start of diversion route for overheight vehicles

Diagram 818.4

NOTES:
(1) Either advisory advance sign or 818.4, or both types of advisory signing, may be used as appropriate.

(2) Continuity signing is essential on the diversion route.

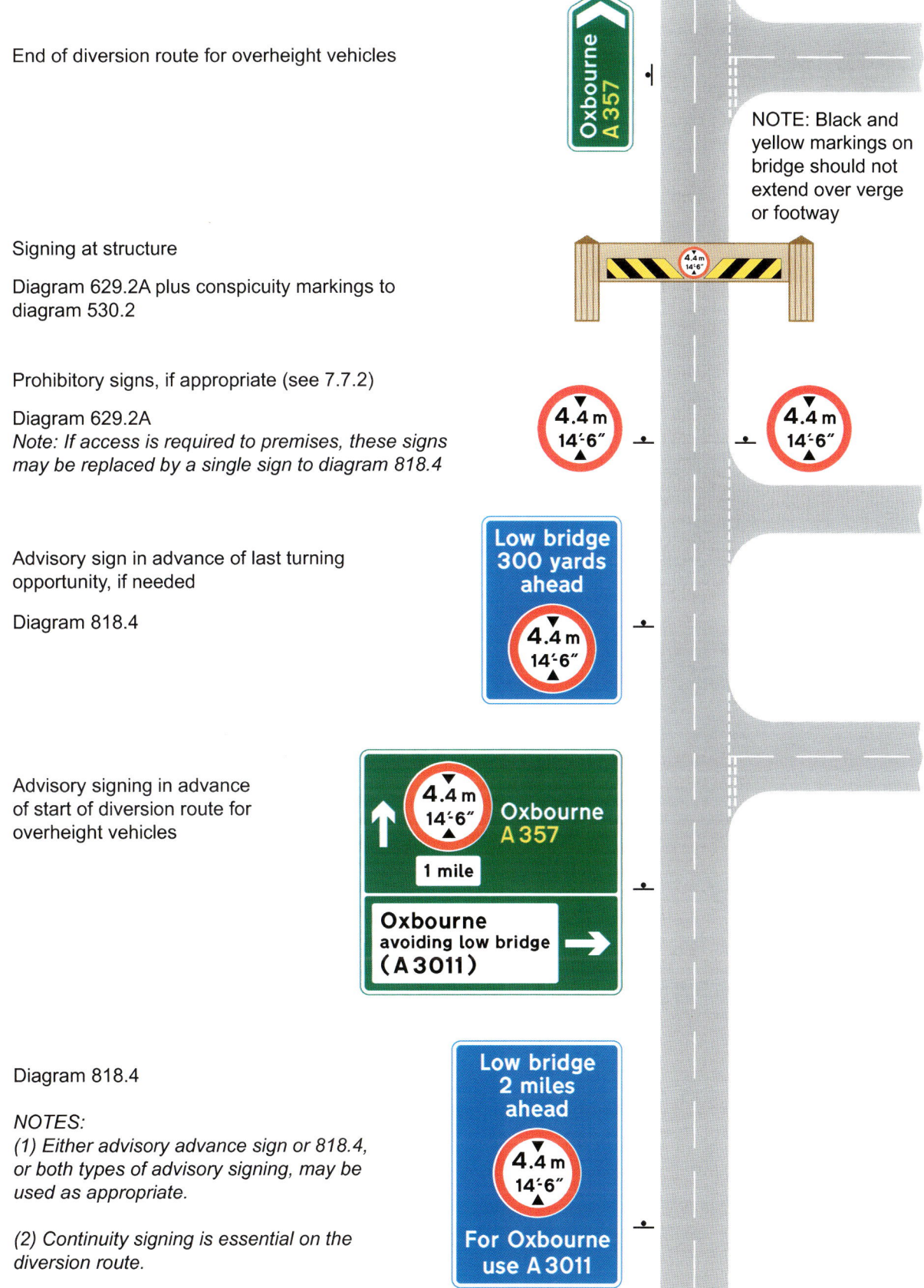

Figure 7-13 Signs on approach to a non-arch bridge with a diversionary route

7.8 Arch bridges

7.8.1. Mandatory signs are not used at arch bridges, as the main risk to these comes from vehicles which, although low enough to pass through the central part of the arch, might strike the curved shoulder of the structure. See Chapter 5 for guidance on the use of road markings at arch bridges.

7.8.2. Arch bridges should be signed using diagram 531.1A (S2-4-3, see **Figure 7-14**) and 531.2 (S2-5-2, see **Figure 7-15**) but see also **7.8.4**. These signs are intended for use in advance of the bridge, and should normally be used on both approaches at the standard siting distances (see **Appendix A**). They should not be used on the bridge itself nor should they be incorporated in directional signs or the sign to diagram 818.5 where diagram 530A (S2-4-2, see **Figure 7-16**) should be used. The signing on the approach to an arch bridge is shown in **Figure 7-17**.

7.8.3. The chord marking or if appropriate the double chord to diagram 532.4 Upper, should be used on the bridge structure. It should always be reflectorised, to make it easier to see at night. If the double chord is used (see **Figure 7-18**), the triangular signs at the side of the arch should be the appropriate size for the road (see **Appendix A**), and those at the top of the arch one size larger. The height indicated on the warning sign to diagram 531.1A will be that for the chord above the centre of the road.

May be used with diagram 531.2 or 572.
The height may be varied.

Figure 7-14 Diagram 531.1A (S2-4-3)
Available headroom at arch bridge ahead

ARCH
BRIDGE
High
vehicles
use middle
of road

May be used only in combination with diagram
531.1A. An arrow may be added to the sign
pointing either to the left or to the right.

Figure 7-15 Diagram 531.2 (S2-5-2)
High vehicles to use the middle of the road
at arch bridge ahead

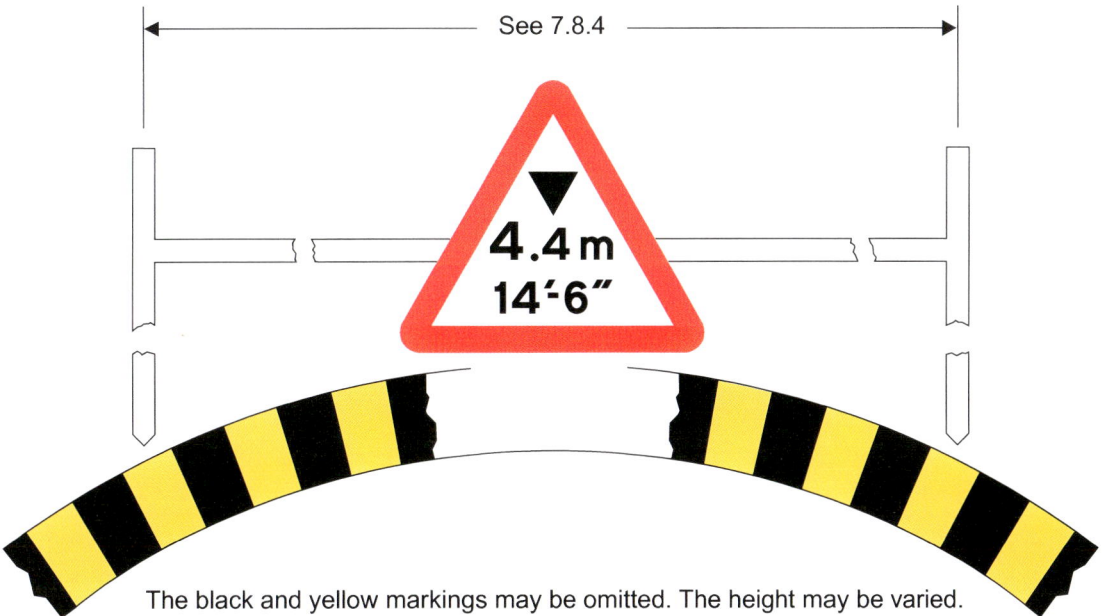

See 7.8.4

▼
4.4 m
14'-6"

The black and yellow markings may be omitted. The height may be varied.

Figure 7-16 Maximum headroom at centre of arch bridge indicated by
a sign to diagram 530A (S2-4-2) plus 532.4 (S2-5-3)

End of diversion route for overheight vehicles

Signing at structure

Diagram 530A plus 532.4

Road markings if needed (see Chapter 5)

Final warning sign

Diagram 531.1A (see 7.8.2)

Diagram 531.2 if needed

Additional sign in advance of last turning opportunity, if needed

Diagram 531.1A plus 572

Advisory signing in advance of start of diversion route for overheight vehicles

Diagram 818.5

NOTES:
(1) Either advisory advance sign or 818.5, or both types of advisory signing, may be used as appropriate.

(2) Continuity signing is essential on the diversion route.

NOTE: Black and yellow markings on bridge should not extend over verge or footway

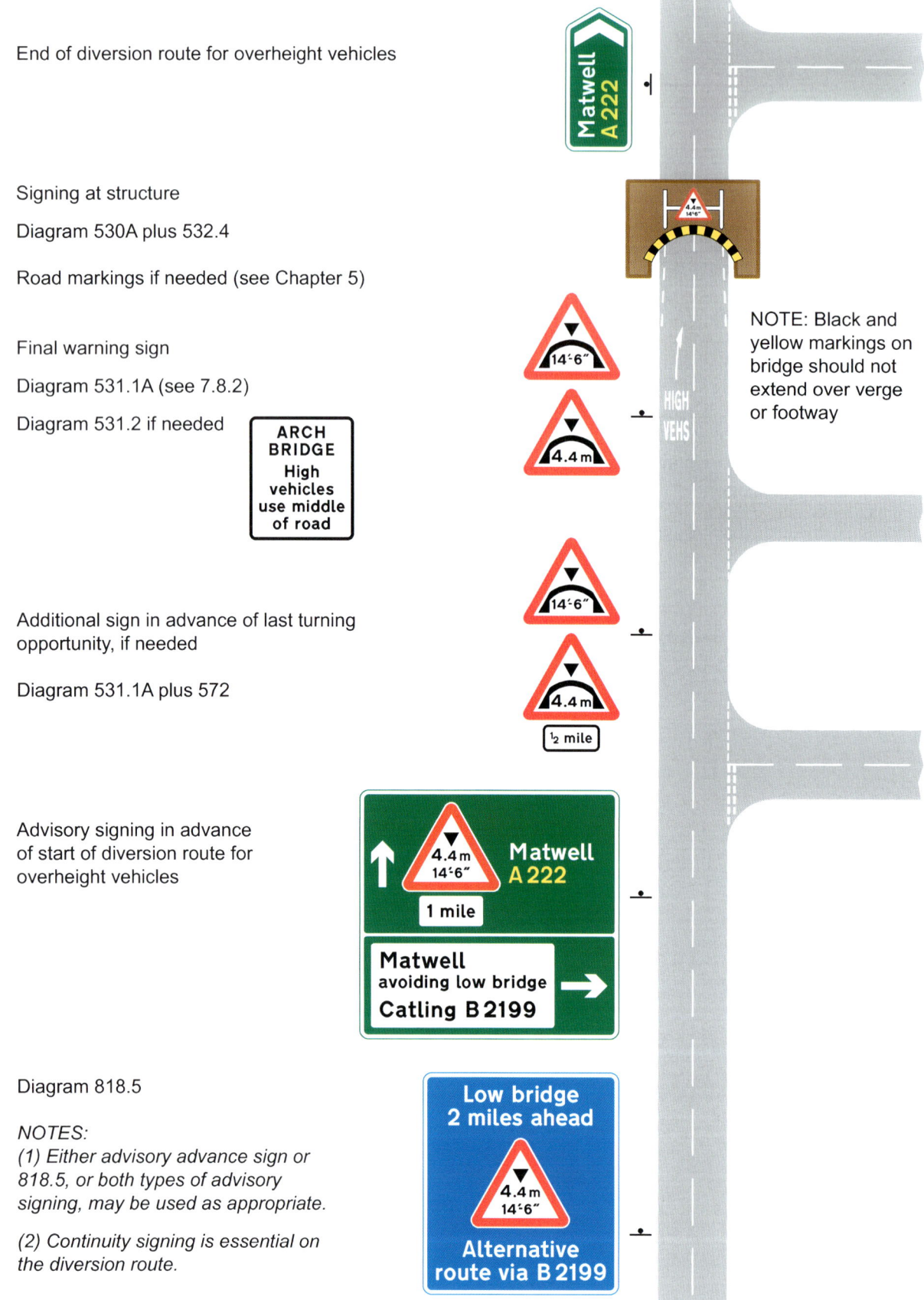

Figure 7-17 Signs on approach to an arch bridge with a diversionary route

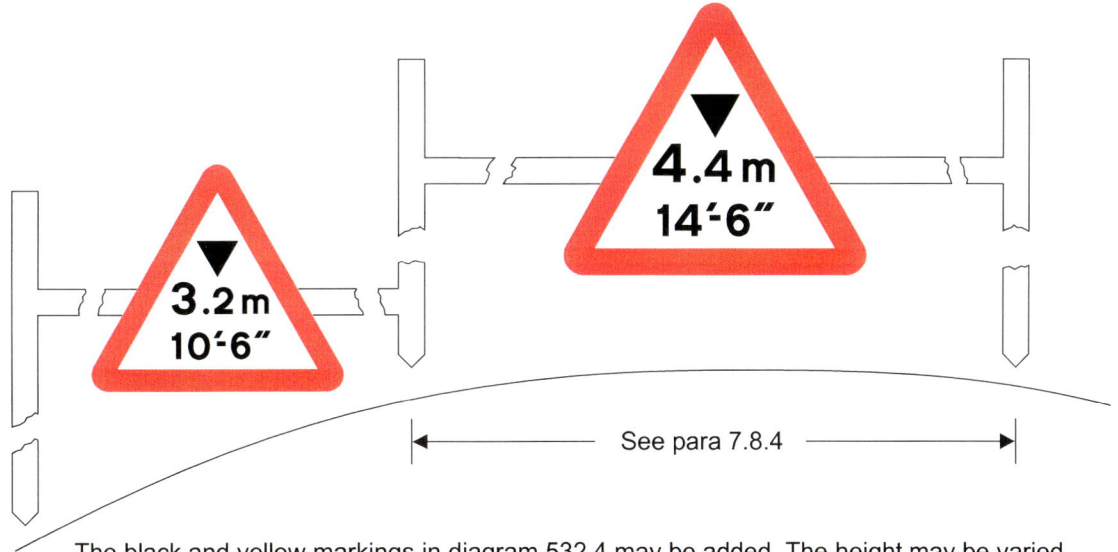

The black and yellow markings in diagram 532.4 may be added. The height may be varied.

Figure 7-18 Maximum headroom at side and in centre of arch bridge
indicated by signs to diagram 530A plus 532.4

7.8.4. The chord marking should indicate the available headroom over a width of not less than 3 metres. The height indicated on the warning signs, determined in accordance with **7.3.3** to **7.5.1**, should be the lowest headroom between the chord limits. On a narrow bridge where the headroom decreases rapidly away from the centre, a 3 metre chord marking is appropriate. On a wide bridge with only a gradual reduction in headroom it might be possible to increase the chord width to 6 metres or more without excessively restricting the signed height, thus maintaining two-way operation for all vehicles that can pass under the bridge. In these circumstances, the warning sign to diagram 531.1A is unlikely to require the supplementary plate to diagram 531.2. Where 16'-6" (5.03 m) headroom is available over much of the carriageway width, but not all of it, diagram 532.4 should be used with the central sign varied to 16'-6" (5.0 m) and the signs on the side chords indicating the clearance available at the near side channel (see **7.3.5** and **7.4.1** for measurement of clearances). Black and yellow markings shown in diagram 532.4 should then be used over those parts of the carriageway where the clearance is below 16'-6", to give greater emphasis to the restricted height. It is recommended that the yellow parts of the marking should be retroreflective; they may also be fluorescent (see **7.3.1**). The chord markings shown in diagrams 532.4 may be used in circumstances other than described above, particularly on wide roads where there are two lanes in one or both directions, with the side chord positioned over the left hand lane. Side chords are also useful where vehicles with a height well below that shown for the centre of the road might strike the bridge if keeping close to the left hand side of the carriageway.

7.9 Composite bridges

7.9.1. Some bridges originally built as arches have been adapted with the addition of girders or beams. Where the arch is the lowest part, the whole structure should be signed as an arch bridge. Black and yellow striped plates (to highlight the profile of the arch) should be suspended from the bridge beam, together with further plates on the arch itself.

7.9.2. Where the beam is lower than any part of the arch, the whole structure should be signed as a non-arch bridge and plates with black and yellow markings to diagram 530.2 suspended from the arch at the height of the beam. Similarly, where two adjacent beam bridges have different headroom, the plates should be located on the higher bridge at the height of the lower one.

7.9.3. Experience has shown that these suspended plates will themselves be struck from time to time and that rigidly-mounted aluminium substrates are not suitable. Rubber or other flexible material should be used for the backing, suspended by means of chains or hinges fixed securely to the bridge structure by a method agreed with the bridge owner. The plates should not be fixed rigidly by screws or bolts to the face of the bridge, as there is a greater risk than with flexibly-suspended plates of them being dislodged and falling onto vehicles on the road beneath. The use of rubber-backed plates will help to avoid annoyance to nearby residents from the noise of hanging metal plates striking the bridge structure in wind or vehicle slipstream. It is recommended that the yellow parts of the marking should be retroreflective; they may also be fluorescent (see 7.3.1). When the signs are lit, the plates should also be lit whenever practicable. This is particularly helpful where a girder bridge is followed by a more restrictive arch bridge.

7.10 Overhanging buildings

7.10.1. Where an overhanging building or other structure causes a restriction over part of the carriageway, the plate to diagram 530.1 should be used with diagram 530A (S2-4-2, see **Figure 7-19**). A distance may be added. Where the building is in another road, an arrow may be added, pointing horizontally to the left or to the right.

May be used with diagram 530.1, 530.2 or 572.
The height may be varied.

Figure 7-19 Diagram 530A (S2-4-2)
Single sign showing available headroom
in both metric and imperial units

May be used only in combination with diagram
530A. A distance, an arrow pointing to the left
or right or both may be added. "building" may
be varied to "buildings" or to "structure"

Figure 7-20 Diagram 530.1 (S2-5-1)
Building overhanging part of a carriageway

8 PEDESTRIANS

8.1 Pedestrian crossings

8.1.1. See Chapter 6 for detailed guidance on pedestrian crossings. The sign to diagram 544 (S14-2-30, see **Figure 8-1**) is for use only at Zebra and Parallel crossings. Zebra and Parallel crossings should not be installed on roads where the 85th percentile speed is 35 mph or more. Diagram 544 must not be used at Puffin or Toucan crossings, where diagram 543 is appropriate, nor where pedestrians cross the road but no formal crossing exists. In the latter case, on high-speed roads, diagram 562 may be used together with the "Pedestrians crossing" supplementary plate and a distance may be added (see **16.1.4**).

Figure 8-1 Diagram 544 (S14-2-30)
Zebra or Parallel crossing ahead

8.1.2. Diagram 544 may be used in combination with a distance plate when it is necessary to site it at a distance much different to that specified in **Appendix A**. When the crossing is in another road leading from a junction ahead, a plate to diagram 547.8, with or without a distance, may be used.

8.1.3. Signs to diagram 544 should be used only when the visibility of the crossing is impaired by a bend or a hump in the road. Signs should not be needed if the visibility of both beacons at a Zebra crossing is greater than the distance shown in **Table 8-1**. If the sight lines to a Zebra crossing are obscured by parked vehicles, the making of a waiting prohibition order should be considered.

Table 8-1 Diagram 544 "Zebra or Parallel crossing ahead" sign criteria

Speed limit (mph)	Visibility distance of both beacons (m)
30	45
40	90

8.2 Vulnerable pedestrians

8.2.1. Where pedestrians frequently use a road without proper footways, diagram 544.1 (S2-2-23, see **Figure 8-2**) may be used to warn drivers of the likely presence of pedestrians in the carriageway. If a footway stops and resumes after some interval, a 'no footway for distance indicated' supplementary plate may be used, with the distance varied to show the length of the road which is without a footway.

8.2.2. The sign to diagram 544.2 (S2-2-24, see **Figure 8-3**) is used to warn of the likely presence of frail or disabled people. Its use should be restricted to sites where relatively high numbers of slow-moving pedestrians are likely to cross a road other than at a Zebra or signalled crossing. This might be near sheltered housing or nursing homes, where drivers need to be reminded that a pedestrian in the road ahead might be frail or blind and need more time to cross than an able-bodied person would.

8.2.3. Where appropriate, the sign to diagram 544.2 (S2-2-24, see **Figure 8-4**)) may be accompanied by a supplementary plate indicating "Disabled people" or "Blind people" (see **Figure 8-5**). A distance, an arrow (pointing horizontally to the left or to the right) or both may be added. Details are given on the working drawings (see **1.16.1**).

May be used with a distance, an arrow
or both, or "No footway for" and a distance

Figure 8-2 Diagram 544.1 (S2-2-23)
Pedestrians in road ahead

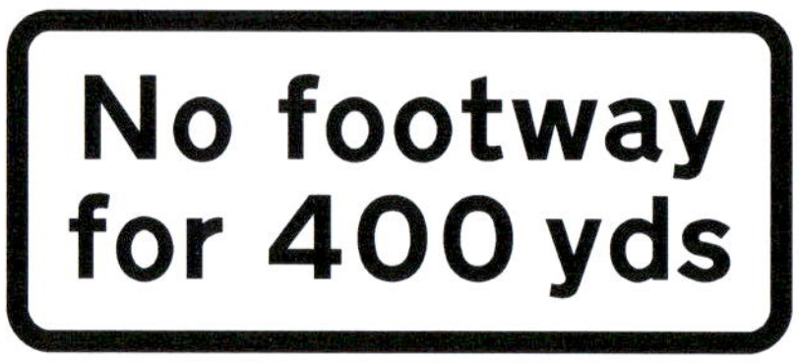

No footway
for 400 yds

May be used only in combination with diagram
544.1 or 545. The distance may be varied.

Figure 8-3 No footway for
distance indicated (S2-2-23)

May be used with a distance, an arrow or both,
"Disabled people" or "Blind people" with or
without a distance and with or without arrow

Figure 8-4 Diagram 544.2 (S2-2-24) Frail or
disabled pedestrians likely to cross the road ahead

May be used only in combination with diagram 544.2.
"Disabled" may be varied to "Blind". A distance, an arrow
pointing to the left or right or both may be added

Figure 8-5 Disabled pedestrians likely
to cross the road ahead (S2-2-24)

8.3 Children

8.3.1. The sign to diagram 545 (S2-2-25, see **Figure 8-6**) is used to warn of the likelihood of encountering children in the road ahead, going to a school or playground. It must be used in combination with one of the supplementary plates shown in **Figure 8-7** to **Figure 8-10**. When used in combination with the "School", "Patrol" or "Disabled children" (and its variants) plates it may also be combined with the light signals shown in diagram 4004 (S14-2-23, see **Figure 8-11**). It should be sited to ensure adequate warning is given; this might require a greater distance than specified in **Appendix A** for signs warning of fixed hazards. A distance, an arrow (pointing to the left or to the right) or both may be added to the plate in accordance with the working drawings.

8.3.2. When combined with "School" or "Patrol", the sign may be provided where children cross the road on their way to or from school, or from one part of a school to another. In most cases they should be restricted to the immediate area outside of a school or where significant numbers of children cross away from a school. If the school or playground caters exclusively or predominantly for disabled, blind or deaf children, the associated plate (see **Figure 8-10**) should be used with the sign to diagram 545. "Disabled children" may be varied to "Blind children" or "Deaf children".

Figure 8-6 Diagram 545 (S2-2-25) Children going to or from school or playground ahead

Figure 8-7 School ahead (S2-2-25)

Figure 8-8 Children's playground ahead (S2-2-25)

Figure 8-9 School crossing patrol ahead (S2-2-25)

Figure 8-10 Disabled children likely to cross the road ahead (S2-2-25)

8.3.3. Where children going to school use roads without footways, it may be necessary to warn drivers of their likely presence in the road. A sign to diagram 545 may be used with "No footway for" distance supplementary plate (see **Figure 8-3**).

8.3.4. When used with the "Patrol" plate the sign to diagram 545 warns of a crossing place where children are supervised by a warden appointed by the local authority and operating with the sign to diagram 605.3, the School Crossing Patrol Sign. "Patrol" signs should not be used at signalled, Zebra or Parallel crossings, as drivers expect to stop whether or not a warden is present.

8.4 Flashing amber lights

8.4.1. Flashing amber lights to diagram 4004 are used to give emphasis to the warning sign where the 85th percentile speed exceeds 35 mph, or on a busy road where a driver's attention is likely to be fully occupied (see **Figure 8-11**). The lights may be used only when diagram 545 is used together with a "School", "Patrol" or "Disabled children" (or its variants) plate and the crossing point is in use (whether or not it is supervised). Lights should not be used near level crossings, traffic signals, Puffin, Toucan, Zebra or Parallel Crossings if this might cause confusion or distraction. They should never be used to warn of children crossing at Zebra, Parallel or signalled crossings.

8.4.2. Where conditions at a patrol site justify flashing lights and there is another patrol site situated within 500 metres that does not, consideration should be given to the provision of lights at both or neither site.

8.4.3. On single carriageway roads with a speed limit of 30 mph at a patrol site with flashing lights, the "School" supplementary plate may be substituted for the plate to diagram 545.1. This plate must be mounted in conjunction with flashing lights to diagram 4004 (see **Figure 8-12**), and may not be varied. It is unlikely to be effective on roads with speed limits greater than 30 mph, or on dual carriageways.

Figure 8-11 Diagram 4004 (S14-2-23)
Flashing amber lights (Alternative types)

Figure 8-12 Part-time advisory 20 mph speed limit at or near a school (S14-2-69)

8.5 Humped crossings

8.5.1. Zebra and Parallel Crossings may be installed on road humps. Diagram 547.8 (S14-2-31, see **Figure 8-13**) may be used together with a sign to diagram 543 (S14-2-28, see Chapter 6) or 544 (see **Figure 8-1**) as appropriate. Further guidance on signing road humps is in section **12**.

"Humped crossing" may be varied to "Zebra crossing", "Parallel Crossing" or omitted.
The distance may be varied or omitted and the arrow reversed to point to the right or omitted

Figure 8-13 Diagram 547.8 (S14-2-31) Zebra crossing
or signal-controlled crossing on road hump ahead

9 ANIMALS AND FARM TRAFFIC

9.1 General

9.1.1. The signs in this section are used to give warning of wild animals, farm animals, horses being taken or ridden along or across a road, or of straying animals from neighbouring unfenced land. The onus is normally on those in charge of farm animals or horses to ensure that their movement is carried out safely; nevertheless the signs may be used at places where animals regularly cross or move along a road, and where visibility is poor.

9.1.2. Where a sign is provided, but the danger is not likely to be present throughout the year (e.g. in winter months when animals are not normally driven across a particular road) traffic authorities should arrange for the sign to be covered during that time, in order to preserve its credibility.

9.1.3. If animals will be encountered only over a known, determinate length of road, the addition of a distance plate, e.g. "For 500 yds" will be appropriate, but the signs may need to be repeated if the danger exists over a considerable distance. It will often be found that animals wander onto the highway not at completely random points, but in particular areas and warning signs should be erected accordingly. See section **17** for further guidance on the use of distance plates.

9.2 Cattle crossing

9.2.1. The cattle sign to diagram 548 (S14-2-41, see **Figure 9-1**) will generally provide sufficient warning of cattle crossings. However, at sites with restricted visibility or where heavy traffic flows make it difficult to herd cattle across the road, the sign to diagram 4005 (S14-2-25, see **Figure 9-2**) (which comprises flashing amber lights and the sign to diagram 548) may be used.

9.2.2. A warning sign and plate to diagram 548.1A (S14-2-41, see **Figure 9-3**) must be used in advance of a cattle crossing where flashing lamps are used.

9.2.3. Such signing is not intended as a solution for anticipated problems on planned new roads, major improvements, or where at other sites the movement of cattle would frequently obstruct traffic for a period of more than three minutes. Nor is a surface crossing appropriate where the traffic flow exceeds 30,000 vehicles per day. In such cases other measures such as a segregating facility should be considered.

9.2.4. Criteria for the provision of flashing amber lights are set out in **Table 9-1**. These are based on the minimum desirable stopping sight distance specified in TD 9, in Volume 6 of DMRB. Lights are not recommended unless the driver's field of clear visibility is less than the distance shown, or the traffic flow exceeds 10,000 vehicles per day on roads where the 85th percentile speed exceeds 30 mph.

9.2.5. Where conditions at a cattle crossing site meet these criteria and, on the same road within approximately half a mile there is another site which does not meet them, consideration should be given to the provision of flashing lamps at both sites.

9.2.6. The flashing lamp units should be erected on both approaches as close as practicable to the start and finish points of the cattle crossing. The mid-point between the flashing lamps must be between 2.4 m and 4 m above the adjacent carriageway. This allows a minimum headroom of 2.1 m to be maintained when the assembly is mounted over a footway.

May be used with a supplementary plate "For" and a distance

Figure 9-1 Diagram 548 (S2-2-27) Cattle likely to be in road ahead

Must be used only in conjunction with diagram 548.1A placed in advance of this sign

Figure 9-2 Diagram 4005 (S14-2-25) Cattle crossing lies ahead and may be in use

The distance may be varied and an arrow may be added pointing to the left or to the right

Figure 9-3 Diagram 548.1A (S14-2-41) Supervised cattle crossing ahead

Table 9-1 Criteria for cattle crossing places

85th percentile speed (mph)	Visibility distance (m)
Up to 30	70
31 to 40	110
41 to 50	150
51 to 60	200
Over 60	Not suitable

9.3 Other animal signs

9.3.1. Signs to diagram 549 ("Sheep", see **Figure 9-4**), 550 ("Wild horses", see **Figure 9-5**) and 551 ("Wild animals", see **Figure 9-6**) may be used wherever such animals are likely to be found in the road (see also **9.1.3**). The signs may be plated for "For" and a distance.

Figure 9-4 Diagram 549 (S2-2-28) Sheep likely to be in road ahead

Figure 9-5 Diagram 550 (S2-2-29) Wild horses likely to be in road ahead

Figure 9-6 Diagram 551 (S2-2-32) Wild animals likely to be in road ahead

9.3.2. Diagram 550.1 (S2-2-30, see **Figure 9-7**) warns of accompanied or ridden horses or ponies (as opposed to wild horses or ponies indicated by the sign to diagram 550) where numbers of horses are frequently walked or ridden along or cross over the road. Warning of horses crossing the road ahead, e.g. where a bridleway crosses the road, can be given by adding a distance plate (with an arrow if the crossing is in another road). Similarly, diagram 550.2 (S2-2-31, see **Figure 9-8**) is used to warn of horse-drawn vehicles in the road ahead.

Figure 9-7 Diagram 550.1 (S2-2-30)
Accompanied horses or ponies likely
to be in the road ahead

Figure 9-8 Diagram 550.2 (S2-2-31)
Horse-drawn vehicles likely
to be in the road ahead

9.3.3. Use of diagram 550.1 to indicate an informal crossing place should normally be considered only where the visibility distance is less than specified in **Table 9-2**. These distances are based on one step below the minimum desirable stopping sight distance (see **9.2.4**).

Table 9-2 Criteria for horse crossing places

85th percentile speed (mph)	Visibility distance (m)
Up to 40	80
41 to 50	110
51 to 60	150
Over 60	200

9.3.4. The sign to diagram 551.1 (S13-2-1, see **Figure 9-9**) may be used only at a site which is approved as a migratory toad crossing. A list of currently approved sites is available from the Froglife Trust (www.froglife.org). The sign may be accompanied by a "for" and a distance plate. It should be displayed only during the migratory period. Signs should be removed or covered at other times of the year; it is recommended that flap-type signs be used to facilitate this.

9.3.5. The sign to diagram 551.2 (S2-2-33, see **Figure 9-10**) may be used where wild fowl are habitually found in the road, such as sites near ponds and watercourses. It may be combined with "For" a distance plate, e.g. "For 150 yds".

Figure 9-9 Diagram 551.1 (S13-2-1)
Migratory toad crossing ahead

Figure 9-10 Diagram 551.2 (S2-2-33)
Wild fowl likely to be in road ahead

9.4 Cattle grids

9.4.1. A cattle grid on a public road should always be preceded by the cattle grid warning sign to diagram 552 (S2-2-35, see **Figure 9-11**), as it might otherwise catch drivers unaware. Grids are especially hazardous for two-wheeled traffic. Signs should normally be sited at the standard distances set out in **Appendix A**. The "horse drawn vehicles and animals" plate with an arrow indicating the direction of the by-pass for horse-drawn vehicles or accompanied animals

(S2-2-35, see **Figure 9-12**) can accompany the sign if the entrance to the by-pass is reasonably close to the grid. Otherwise a duplicate sign to diagram 552 and "horse drawn vehicles and animals" plate should be placed at the entrance, with a distance plate mounted directly below the triangular sign indicating the distance to the grid. If the grid is in another road, the advance warning sign should be accompanied by a distance plate with arrow.

Figure 9-11 Diagram 552 (S2-2-35)
Cattle grid ahead

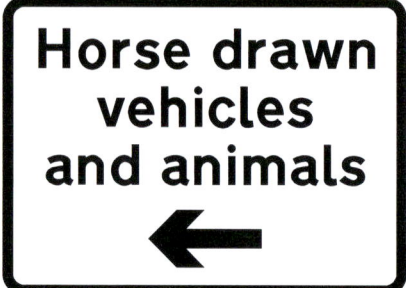

Figure 9-12 By-pass of cattle grid (S2-2-35)

9.5 Farm traffic

9.5.1. The sign to diagram 553.1 (S2-2-34, see **Figure 9-13**) may be used wherever farm tractors or other agricultural vehicles frequently travel in the road at low speed, turn into or out of an entrance or cross a road. It may be particularly appropriate where visibility of an access or of turning vehicles is inadequate, or where such vehicles turn unexpectedly across high-speed roads. The sign must always be used with a plate which may read "Farm traffic", "Wide vehicles" or "Tractors turning" (see **Figure 9-14**). Where there are two entrances between which vehicles regularly travel, an indication of the distance over which the hazard extends may be added to the plate, e.g. "for 250 yds".

May be used only in combination
with the plate illustrated in figure 9-14

Figure 9-13 Diagram 553.1 (S2-2-34)
Agricultural vehicles likely to be in road ahead

May be used only in combination
with diagram 553.1

Figure 9-14 Agricultural vehicles (S2-2-34)

9.6 Gates

9.6.1. The sign to diagram 554B (S2-2-36, see **Figure 9-15**) or 554C (S2-2-37, see **Figure 9-16**) as appropriate may be used in a road which has gates installed, usually for the control of farm animals. As drivers are likely to have to stop in order to open the gate, diagram 554B "Gate" should normally be supplemented by a distance plate. A plate "For" and a distance, e.g. "For 2 miles" may be used with diagram 554C "Gates".

Figure 9-15 Diagram 554B (S2-2-36)
Gate ahead

Figure 9-16 Diagram 554C (S2-2-37)
Gates ahead

10.1 Fords and floods

10.1.1. The "Ford" sign to diagram 554 (S2-2-38, see **Figure 10-1**) should be used at all fords, even those which dry up in summer. The sign should also be placed at the entry to the road leading to the ford, accompanied by a distance plate with or without an arrow as appropriate (see section **17**). Where a road is subjected to frequent flooding, the "Ford" sign may be supplemented by a "Road liable to flooding" plate. Whilst the water depth gauge is no longer a prescribed sign, authorities are encouraged to continue to place these indications at locations where the ford might become impassable in times of flood.

10.1.2. The "Flood" sign to diagram 554A (S13-2-2, see **Figure 10-2**) may be displayed only for as long as the hazard continues to exist or is expected to recur in the near future. It may be accompanied by a distance plate with or without an arrow as appropriate and should be followed, beyond the flooded length of road, by a "Try your brakes" sign to diagram 554.1 (S2-2-39, see **Figure 10-3**). If the water depth makes the road impassable, a "ROAD AHEAD CLOSED" sign, placed at each end of the closure at junctions where traffic can be diverted, would be more appropriate.

May be used with a distance with or without an arrow pointing to the left or right

Figure 10-1 Diagram 554 (S2-2-38) Ford ahead

May be used with a distance plate with or without an arrow pointing to the left or right or an arrow pointing to the left or right

Figure 10-2 Diagram 554A (S13-2-2) Flood ahead

May be used with hill signs, "Keep in low gear" plate or the sign to diagram 817.2

Figure 10-3 Diagram 554.1 (S2-2-39) Try your brakes

10.1.3. The "Try your brakes" sign should also be installed on the exit side of a ford. Given the likely minor status of the road, adequate warning is usually provided if these signs are mounted on the reverse of the "Ford" signs.

10.1.4. This sign may also be used with signs associated with steep hills and escape lanes (see section **6**). The largest size (1500 mm) could be used in these instances, but not at fords.

10.1.5. Depth gauges should be provided at fords or locations where flooding is known to be a persistent problem (see **Figure 10-4**). The zero level is the lowest part of the carriageway. Gauges should be sited so that the depth of water can be seen by road users on both approaches. These are not prescribed by the Regulations and need to be authorised by the appropriate national authority.

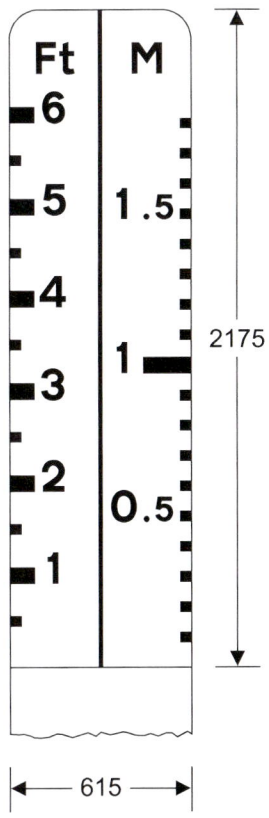

Figure 10-4 Depth gauge

10.2 Ice and snow

10.2.1. The "Ice" sign to diagram 554.2 (S13-2-4, see **Figure 10-5**), and supplementary plates "Ice" or "Snowdrifts" (S13-2-4, see **Figure 10-6**), are temporary signs used when a route is unusually dangerous as a result of extensive icing or heavy snowfalls. The signs must be removed when conditions return to normal. When indicating "Ice", one size larger x-height should be used to compensate for the short word, which would otherwise result in a very small plate. "Snowdrifts" should be at the normal x-height for the road (see **Appendix B**).

10.2.2. The "Ice" or "Snowdrifts" plate must never be used alone. It must be used with one of the following signs: 554.2, 622.1A (goods vehicle weight limit), 622.4 (No articulated vehicles), 629A (width limit), 629.1 (length limit) or 632 (no overtaking). The regulatory signs are used when snow or ice conditions make it unsafe for the prohibited type of vehicle to use the road, or where, in the case of diagram 632, overtaking would be hazardous.

Figure 10-5 Diagram 554.2 (S13-2-4)
Risk of ice or packed snow ahead

Figure 10-6 Ice ahead (S13-2-4)

10.3 Quaysides and water courses

10.3.1. The quayside or river bank sign to diagram 555 (S2-2-40, see **Figure 10-7**) should be used wherever a public road approaches an unbarriered quayside or river bank. In order to break up the straight ahead view at such locations and to give greater emphasis, hazard markers to diagram 560, chevrons to diagram 515, or appropriate direction signs may be mounted to face traffic that might be at risk.

10.3.2. The water course sign, diagram 555.1 (S2-2-41, see **Figure 10-8**), is intended for locations where a road runs alongside a water course of sufficient depth to be a danger if a vehicle leaves the carriageway. This may be important if the water surface cannot easily be seen, e.g. because of obscuration by vegetation, or if the road is liable to flooding and there is difficulty in distinguishing between carriageway and water course. A sign is not necessary if the road edge is kerbed or if a safety fence is provided. Where the risk is to vehicles parking alongside a water course, e.g. at a quayside, diagram 555 will be more appropriate.

May be used with a distance plate with or without an arrow pointing to the left or right or an arrow pointing to the left or right

Figure 10-7 Diagram 555 (S2-2-40)
Quayside or river bank

May be used with "For" and a distance plate. The symbol may be reversed

Figure 10-8 Diagram 555.1 (S2-2-41)
Water course alongside road

11 ROAD SURFACE

11.1 Uneven road

11.1.1. The uneven road sign, diagram 556 (S13-2-5, see **Figure 11-1**), is used to warn of danger arising from longitudinal or transverse irregularities in the road surface which at the normal speed of traffic might seriously impair control of a vehicle. The use of this sign should generally be regarded as temporary, pending remedial work to the carriageway. It should be removed when the defect has been remedied. A plate to diagram 511 "REDUCE SPEED NOW" and also a plate "For" and a distance may be used with it. The uneven road sign should not be used at level crossings where the rail levels make the road uneven; diagram 782 is used for this purpose.

Figure 11-1 Diagram 556 (S13-2-5)
Uneven road ahead

11.2 Soft verges

11.2.1. The soft verges sign, diagram 556.1 (S2-2-42, see **Figure 11-2**) and the associated supplementary plate "Soft verges" (S2-2-42, see **Figure 11-3**), should never be used simply to discourage parking (see Chapter 3 for verge and footway parking). It is intended to deal with problems where driving on the verge can damage drains or might result in vehicles becoming stuck or damaging the verge. For lengths greater than two miles, the sign should be repeated at intervals of approximately one mile.

May be used only in combination
with the plate illustrated in figure 11-3

Figure 11-2 Diagram 556.1 (S2-2-42)
Soft verges ahead

Soft verges for 2 miles

May be used only in combination with
diagram 556.1, the distance may be
varied or "for" and the distance omitted

Figure 11-3 Soft verges for
distance indicated (S2-2-42)

11.3 Slippery road

11.3.1. The slippery road sign, diagram 557 (S13-2-6, see **Figure 11-4**), is intended for use where the danger of vehicles skidding is greater than normal. A plate "For" and a distance may be used with this sign. The degree of danger cannot be precisely defined as this depends upon the skid resistance value, speed of traffic and the degree of superelevation on bends. It is for the traffic authority to judge whether overall conditions are sufficiently sub-standard that special warning is necessary. Detailed guidance can be found in HD 28, Skidding Resistance, in Volume 7 of DMRB. Care must be taken not to over-use the sign, or its credibility will be undermined. Remedial works to improve the skidding resistance of the road surface or to improve drainage should be undertaken as soon as practicable and the signs removed on completion of the works.

Figure 11-4 Diagram 557 (S13-2-6)
Slippery road ahead

11.4 Loose chippings

11.4.1. Loose chippings arising from surface dressing operations can pose a hazard either due to being thrown up into the path of oncoming vehicles or by causing vehicles to skid on the loose surface. While works are taking place, the sign to diagram 7009 (S13-2-10, see **Figure 11-5**) should be used together with the supplementary plate to diagram 513.2 (S13-4-2, see **Figure 11-6**), varied to indicate a recommended maximum speed of 10 mph. On completion of the works, the sign may be retained for so long as the traffic authority considers it necessary to warn drivers in which case the supplementary plate should be replaced by the plates comprising sign diagram 7009.1 (S13-4-3, see **Figure 11-7**). It is not permitted to vary the recommended speed on this sign. Further advice on signing during surface dressing operations can be found on the Road Surface Treatments Association's website at www.rsta-uk.org.

May be used with diagram 513.2, a plate "For" and a distance or a distance with or without an arrow pointing to the left or right, an arrow on its own or 7009.1

Figure 11-5 Diagram 7009 (S13-2-10)
Loose chippings on road ahead

Skid risk

Max speed 10

May be used only in combination with diagram 7009 (or 512.1, 512.2, 513; see section 3). The speed may be varied

Figure 11-6 Diagram 513.2 (S13-4-2)
Maximum speed advised

Max speed 20

May be used only in combination with diagram 7009. The speed must not be varied

Figure 11-7 Diagram 7009.1 (S13-4-3)
Risk of skidding and maximum speed 20 mph advised on road with loose chippings

12 ROAD HUMPS

12.1 General

12.1.1. Diagram 557.1 (S2-2-43, see **Figure 12-1**) is used to warn of the presence of a road hump or a series of humps. It must be accompanied by one of the plates shown. The plates must not be used alone. However, no signs are required to warn of humps in a 20 mph zone signed with traffic signs to diagram 674 (Highways (Road Humps) Regulations 1999). In Northern Ireland, refer to the Road Humps Regulations (Northern Ireland) 1999 and, in Scotland, the Road Humps (Scotland) Regulations 1998.

12.1.2. In 20 mph zones signed with diagram 674, road markings are not required on road humps, speed cushions or thumps; however they may be used if the traffic authority considers them appropriate. Hump markings are always required where a 20 mph speed limit is signed using diagram 670 (see Chapter 3).

May be used only in combination with the plates illustrated in
Figure 12-2, **Figure 12-3** or **Figure 12-4** and with the marking to diagram 1062

Figure 12-1 Diagram 557.1 (S2-2-43)
Road hump of series of road humps ahead

12.1.3. Individual circumstances will determine whether signs for road humps should be provided on both sides of the road. Where a gateway is to be used as a speed-reducing feature in advance of humps, signs on both sides of the carriageway, incorporated into the gateway could be considered. Further advice on siting can be found in **Appendix A**.

12.1.4. Where several adjoining roads have humps, the distance on the sign plates should relate to the humps on the road on which the sign is erected. Separate signing for adjoining roads should not be necessary, provided the first hump in the adjoining road, whether it is the major or the minor one, is within 40 metres of the junction of the two roads.

12.1.5. As diagram 557.1 plated with **Figure 12-2** may be installed only on the road with speed control features, a 50 mm x-height is sufficient for the supplementary plate. **Figure 12-3** and **Figure 12-4** when incorporating an arrow, indicate the presence of humps on side roads, and may themselves be used on roads where speeds are higher. A wider range of x-heights is therefore used for these signs (see **Appendix B** for details).

12.1.6. Signing of a humped Zebra, Parallel or signalled crossing in a series of road humps will generally be necessary only if the spacing between it and adjacent humps is greater than 100 metres (see also **8.4.3** for details of sign plates).

12.1.7. **Figure 12-5** illustrates the range of signing that might be used where road humps are installed on adjacent roads within an area. Signs should be considered at each entrance to the area, other than at short culs-de-sac with no humps and fewer than about 100 dwellings. If the humps are spaced more than 150 metres apart, each individual hump should be signed. Similar signing should be used where humps are installed on one road only.

These plates may be used only in combination with diagram 557.1. The distance may be varied and, on **Figure 12-3** and **Figure 12-4** may be omitted. The legend on **Figure 12-4** may be on two lines. On **Figure 12-3** and **Figure 12-4** the arrow may be reversed, or a second arrow pointing in the opposite direction may be added. The arrow on **Figure 12-4** may be omitted; the appropriate x-height will then be 50 mm.

Figure 12-2 Road humps for the distance indicated

Figure 12-3 Road humps in the direction and for the distance indicated

Figure 12-4 Road hump in the direction and at the distance indicated

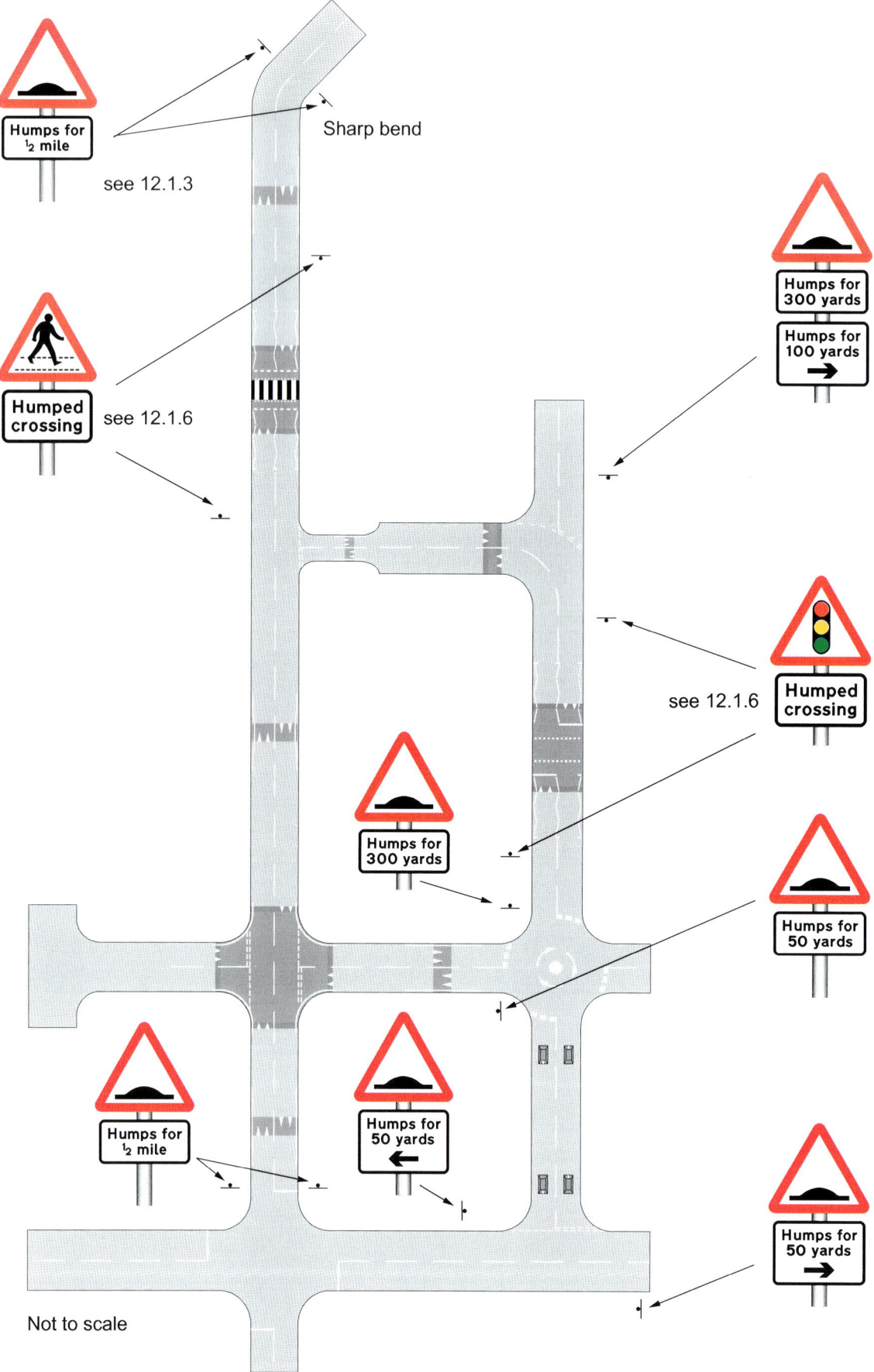

Figure 12-5 Range of signing that might be used where road humps
are installed on adjacent roads within an area

13.1 General

13.1.1. The low-flying aircraft sign, diagram 558 (S2-2-46, see **Figure 13-1**), is for use on roads skirting or in the vicinity of airfields where road users are likely to be startled by low-flying aircraft or by sudden noise from aircraft. A plate indicating "Gliders" (see **Figure 13-2**) should be added where appropriate. A plate to diagram 773 should be mounted below the sign if wig-wag signals are installed to control the movement of traffic during the take-off or landing of aircraft.

13.1.2. The standard siting distances recommended in **Appendix A** are not likely to be appropriate for aircraft warning signs; an aeroplane might be virtually overhead before a driver sees the sign. It will therefore usually be more effective for this sign to be sited further in advance of the flight path, accompanied by "For" and a distance plate (see section **17**). However, in the case of wig-wag signals, signs to diagrams 558 and 773 (see **Figure 20-4**) should be sited at the standard distance from the stop line in addition to any general aircraft warning signs to diagram 558 used in advance. A distance may be added to the "Gliders" plate where this is used; details can be found on the working drawing.

13.1.3. Where helicopters are likely to be encountered, the sign to diagram 558.1 (S2-2-47, see **Figure 13-3**) may be used.

May be used with "Gliders" plate illustrated below, "For" and a distance or diagram 773

Figure 13-1 Diagram 558 (S2-2-46) Low-flying aircraft

May be used only in combination with diagram 558. The legend "for" and a distance may be added

Figure 13-2 Gliders supplementary plate

May be used with plate "For" and a distance

Figure 13-3 Diagram 558.1 (S2-2-47) Low-flying helicopters

14.1 General

14.1.1. The risk of falling or fallen rocks sign, diagram 559 (S2-2-44, see **Figure 14-1**), should be used where there is a danger of rocks falling onto a road. A plate, "For" and a distance, indicating the length of road likely to be affected may be used with the sign. The appropriate variant is used to indicate which side rocks might fall, but where rocks might fall from either side (e.g. in a gorge) the left hand side of the road variant should be used.

Figure 14-1 Diagram 559 (S2-2-44)
Risk of falling or fallen rocks

15 HAZARD MARKERS

15.1 General

15.1.1. Hazard markers to diagram 560 (S2-6-2, see **Figure 15-1**) may be circular or rectangular in shape and are prescribed in three colours. As viewed by the drivers of approaching vehicles these are:

a) red on the left hand edge of the carriageway

b) white on the right hand edge of a single carriageway road

c) amber on the right hand edge of a dual carriageway road adjacent to the central reservation, or a road carrying traffic in one direction only.

15.1.2. The top of the sign must be not less than 550 mm nor more than 1000 mm above the surface of the adjacent carriageway. When mounted on a post specially provided for the purpose, that part of the post which extends above ground level may be:

a) of any single colour, or

b) coloured black and white in alternate horizontal bands, each band being not less than 225 mm nor more than 350 mm deep.

15.1.3. The black and white banded post enhances the conspicuity of the hazard marker. In rural areas or in areas where speeds are high, this type of post will generally be most suitable. In urban areas, or traffic-calmed zones, single-coloured posts may be appropriate.

15.1.4. The markers may be used to indicate the edge of the carriageway on embankments, mountain roads and other points where special danger exists. They may also be used, supplemented where appropriate with signs to diagrams 516 or 517 to indicate a place where the carriageway suddenly narrows or to indicate obstructions such as a bridge parapet, abutment or building unusually near the carriageway edge. In these cases the markers may be fixed directly to the structure instead of to a separate post, but see also diagram 528.1.

15.1.5. The signs must not be illuminated by means of internal or external lighting. They must be illuminated by means of retroreflecting material.

The signs may be coloured red, white or amber and the surface of the rectangular sign may be curved

Figure 15-1 Diagram 560 (S2-6-2)
Hazard at edge of carriageway

15.1.6. Care should be taken to ensure that hazard markers do not appear confusing at night. This may occur for example if headlights (with raised or dipped beams) are reflected from markers delineating more than one bend. It is recommended that, following installation, they are checked at night from a moving vehicle.

15.1.7. The use of hazard markers on safety fences or barriers on high-speed roads is only suitable where their line reliably follows the carriageway edge. Where safety fences do not consistently follow the line of the road edge; mounting reflectors on them is likely to mislead drivers as to the true position of the verge. The recommended method of delineating the road edge is to use edge of carriageway markings (incorporating raised ribs if appropriate) together with road studs. It may sometimes be appropriate to use markers on safety fences on sinuous mountain roads over short lengths, or at sharp bends, where separate posts may be inconvenient. When used in this way, the markers must still conform to the Regulations and to the requirements with respect to colour, size, shape and mounting height. Consideration should also be given to the potential consequences of the fence being struck by a vehicle. If the markers are of heavy construction, they could themselves be hazardous.

16.1 General

16.1.1. Although prescribed mainly for temporary use to warn of transient or occasional hazards such as "Dust cloud" or "Census", diagram 562 (S2-2-56 & S13-2-7, see **Figure 16-1**) is also used for certain permanent features not easily represented symbolically, e.g. "Hidden dip".

16.1.2. The sign conveys no specific message on its own; it must always be accompanied by one of its supplementary plates (S2-2-56 & S13-2-7, see **Figure 16-2**) or diagram 563.1 (S14-2-7, see **Figure 16-3**). Plate legends for permanent signs are given in S2-2-56 and those for temporary situations in S13-2-7. Reference should be made to the working drawings to determine the correct layout of the different legends.

16.1.3. When the legend on the plate indicates a temporary hazard, "Accident", "Census", "Dust cloud", "Fallen tree", "Frost damage", "Overhead cable repairs", "Runners in road", "Smoke" or "Walkers in road", the sign may be retained only for so long as the hazard indicated continues to exist or is expected to recur in the near future.

May be used only in combination with a supplementary plate illustrated below or diagram 563.1

Figure 16-1 Diagram 562 (S2-2-56 & S13-2-7) Other danger ahead

May be used only in combination with diagram 562. "Accident" may be varied to "Ambulance station", "Blasting", "Blind summit", "Census", "Dust cloud", "Fallen tree", "Fire station", "Frost damage", "Hidden dip", "Overhead cable repairs", "Pedestrians crossing", "Rising bollards", "Road liable to flooding", "Runners in road", "Smoke" or "Walkers in road". A distance, an arrow or both may be added

Figure 16-2 Plate showing the nature of the other danger (S2-2-56 & S13-2-7)

16.1.4. When the plate is varied to "Pedestrians crossing", it may be used where pedestrians frequently cross high-speed roads, although no formal provision is made for them, and sited at a distance appropriate to the 85th percentile speed (see **Appendix A**). Such locations may be where new by-passes intersect established pedestrian routes. As the crossing point is unlikely to be apparent to drivers, a distance should normally be added, in accordance with the working drawing. The sign must not be used where a formal crossing, such as a Zebra, Parallel or Toucan Crossing, is provided.

16.2 Wig-wag signals

16.2.1. The sign to diagram 563.1 (S14-2-7, see **Figure 16-3**), in combination with diagram 562, may be used only where wig-wag signals to diagram 3014 (S14-2-5, see Chapter 6) are installed in the vicinity of premises used regularly by fire and rescue authority, Scottish Fire and Rescue Service, police or ambulance vehicles.

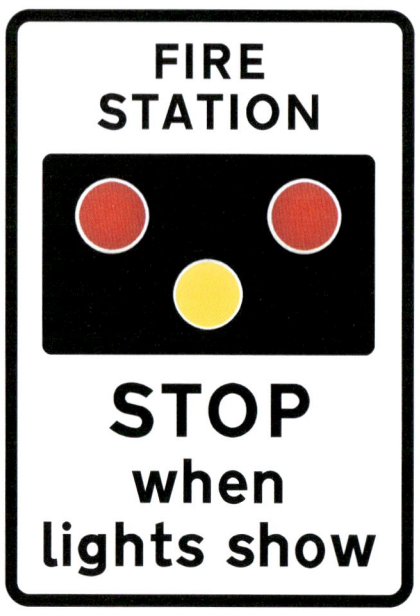

May be used only in combination with diagram 562. "FIRE" may be varied to "AMBULANCE", "POLICE", "FIRE AND AMBULANCE", "FIRE AND POLICE", "POLICE AND AMBULANCE" or "FIRE, POLICE AND AMBULANCE". A distance, an arrow pointing horizontally to the left or right or both may be added

Figure 16-3 Diagram 563.1 (S14-2-7)
Stop when lights show

17 DISTANCE PLATES

17.1 General

17.1.1. These plates may be used with many of the warning signs described in this chapter (as the first associated plate legend in the schedule sign tables). However, many supplementary plates may incorporate distances, obviating the need for separate distance plates. The working drawings show the correct layouts (see **1.16**).

17.1.2. The "For" and a distance plate (see **Figure 17-1**) is used to indicate the distance over which a hazard extends. Generally, if this is for more than two miles, the warning sign should be repeated at suitable intervals with the plate indicating the remaining distance to the end of the hazard. However, account should be taken of visual obstructions en-route e.g. a rock outcrop might hide sheep wandering onto the road, necessitating a sign at that point.

17.1.3. On motorways or other roads with grade separated junctions where the hazard might extend over a long distance, (e.g. wild animals) the warning sign with a "For" and a distance plate should be repeated after every access slip road, or, if this distance would be excessive, at intervals of approximately five miles. Each plate should show the distance remaining to the end of the hazard.

17.1.4. The distance plate (see **Figure 17-2**) indicates the distance ahead to a hazard. The caption below each diagram illustrated in this chapter specifies if a distance plate may be used. Where such a sign is sited at a distance from the hazard significantly different to that recommended in **Appendix A**, it should normally be supplemented with a distance plate.

17.1.5. The distance and an arrow plate (see **Figure 17-3**) is placed in advance of a junction, indicating the distance along the road from that junction to the hazard. The distance is measured from the junction and not from the sign. The sign may be sited on a minor road approaching a junction if the hazard is on the major road. The direction of the arrow may be reversed.

17.1.6. The distance shown on all three plates may be varied with:

a) distances over 3 miles being expressed in miles to the nearest mile;

b) distances of ½ mile or more but less than 3 miles being expressed to the ¼ mile; and

c) distances of less than ½ mile being expressed in yards to the nearest 10 yards. In no circumstances may metric distances be used.

The indication of distance on these signs may be varied (see Appendix C). On the distance and direction plate, the distance may be omitted. The direction of the arrow may be reversed

Figure 17-1	**Figure 17-2**	**Figure 17-3**
Distance over which hazard exists	Distance to hazard	Distance and direction to hazard

18.1 Animal disease

18.1.1. The animal disease sign is prescribed in S13-9-1 and the legend derived from the provisions in S13-9-5 (see **Figure 18-1**) as a temporary sign for use in connection with an outbreak of an animal disease. The appropriate name of the disease should be shown on the sign. It should be erected on roads at the boundaries of infected areas designated under the Animal Health Act 1981 (in Northern Ireland refer to the Diseases of Animals (NI) Order 1981). To assist in proper control of the disease, traffic authorities should ensure that the prescribed warning signs are used. The signs must be removed when the area has been cleared of the disease.

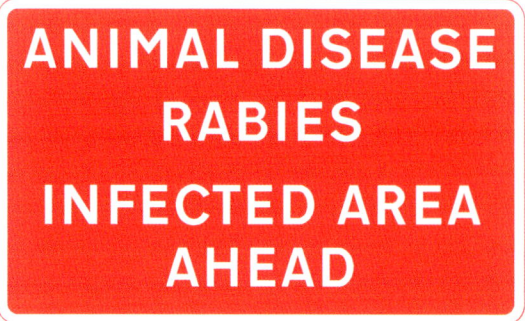

"RABIES" may be omitted or varied to any appropriate animal disease. "AHEAD" may be omitted or varied to "ENDS" or to a horizontal arrow pointing to the left or to the right

Figure 18-1 Area infected by animal disease (S13-9-1)

18.2 Oncoming vehicles

18.2.1. The "Oncoming vehicles in middle of road" plate (S2-2, see **Figure 18-2**) is used where a physical restriction requires large vehicles to be driven in the middle of the road over a short distance. It is not intended to be used where the general width of a road is such that a large vehicle would be forced to straddle the centre line over a long distance. It may be used in combination with the "bend" signs to diagrams 512, 512.1, 512.2, 512.3 and 513 (see **3.1**) and the "road narrows" signs to diagrams 516 and 517 (see section **4**). It might also sometimes be appropriate to use it with the "hump bridge" sign, diagram 528 (see **7.1**) or the "tunnel" sign, diagram 529.1 (see **7.2**). Diagram 531.2 should be used at arch bridges (see **7.8**). Where double white lines (diagram 1013.1) are used, they should be interrupted so that a vehicle is not forced to cross them.

Figure 18-2 Large vehicles in middle of road (S2-2)

18.3 Side winds

18.3.1. The "side winds" sign to diagram 581 (S2-2-45, see **Figure 18-3**) is used where vehicles are suddenly exposed to risk from strong winds. Such locations may include exposed bridges or places where vehicles emerge from cuttings in areas which are particularly prone to high winds. Drivers must anticipate some adverse effects caused by side wind and in order to maintain the effectiveness of this sign, it should not be over-used.

18.3.2. The sign may be used with "For" and a distance plate where an unusual hazard exists over a longer length, e.g. on a viaduct or high embankment. However, it should not normally be used on the open road, where drivers must expect gusts of wind.

Figure 18-3 Diagram 581 (S2-2-45)
Side winds likely ahead

19.1 Military vehicles

19.1.1. The sign to diagram 582 (S2-2-48, see **Figure 19-1**) may be used at locations where military vehicles are expected either to cross the road ahead or to be moving at low speed along the road. If the vehicles have regular entry and exit points along the road, the use of "For" and a distance plate may be appropriate.

19.1.2. The sign is not restricted to warning of tanks; it may be used for any military vehicles which are either larger than might normally be expected along that type of road, or travel at reduced speed.

Figure 19-1 Diagram 582 (S2-2-48)
Slow-moving military vehicles likely
to be crossing or in road ahead

19.2 Slow lorries

19.2.1. The slow-moving vehicles signs, diagram 583 (S2-2-49, see **Figure 19-2**) and the associated plate "Slow lorries for" a distance (S2-2-49, see **Figure 19-3**), are intended for use on roads where the gradient is such as to have an adverse effect on the speed of heavy commercial vehicles, thereby causing a potential hazard to other vehicles in the same lane. This is not simply a question of congestion. The problem can occur even when there is more than one lane. At times of light traffic flow, a vehicle being driven in the left hand lane at 70 mph might close unexpectedly rapidly on a slow-moving lorry, or on a queue of vehicles waiting to pass it.

Must be used only in combination
with "Slow lorries for" and a distance plate

Figure 19-2 Diagram 583 (S2-2-49)
Slow-moving vehicles likely on incline ahead

May be used only in combination with diagram 583.
The distance may be varied and "miles" may be
varied to "mile"

Figure 19-3 Distance over which
slow-moving vehicles hazard exists

19.2.2. The criteria for using these signs will differ from the criteria for normal steep hill signs because they are aimed at drivers following the slow vehicle and not at the driver of the slow vehicle itself. In addition to the gradient of the hill, consideration should be given to the length of the hill and the differential speed of heavy and other traffic. They are most likely to be of use on motorways and high-speed dual carriageway roads with substandard gradients. The sign should be used for uphill traffic only; the "steep hill" signs in section **6** should, if needed, be used in the downhill direction.

19.3 Queues likely

19.3.1. Drivers should expect to meet queues on the approaches to roundabouts or traffic signals, where, if advance warning is needed, it can usually be given using signs to diagram 510 or 543 as appropriate. The queues likely sign, diagram 584 (S2-2-50, see **Figure 19-4**), and associated plate "Queues likely" (S2-2-50, see **Figure 19-5**), are intended for use where drivers might unexpectedly come across a queue, e.g. around a bend or over the brow of a hill. These signs should be used only where there is a persistent problem, causing a significant hazard, despite the presence of the standard warning signs and are not appropriate as a general warning of congestion. They should be sited sufficiently far in advance of the obstruction to the sight line to enable drivers to stop in time. Distance plates must not be used.

19.3.2. Where the queue is likely to be in a road that leads from a junction ahead, the "Queues likely" plate may incorporate an arrow pointing to the left or to the right as appropriate. Details are shown on the working drawing.

19.3.3. The sign may also be used on motorways or other high-speed dual carriageway roads with grade separated junctions where queues on an exit slip road regularly extend back onto the main carriageway. Where queues on the slip road effectively shorten the deceleration length available, but do not usually extend onto the main through carriageway, the variant "Queues likely on slip road" should be used. Care should be taken to ensure that the assembly does not obstruct the driver's view of existing signs.

Must be used only in combination
with "Queues likely" plate

Figure 19-4 Diagram 584 (S2-2-50)
Traffic queues likely on road ahead

Must be used in combination with diagram 584. "Queues likely"
may be varied to "Queues likely on slip road"

Figure 19-5 Queues likely
on road ahead (S2-2-50)

20.1 General

20.1.1. This section gives a brief description of the prescribed traffic signs used at level crossings and tramway crossings. For further guidance, reference should be made to the Office of Rail and Road (ORR) publication 'Railway Safety Publication 7, Level Crossings: A guide for managers, designers and operators' published on the ORR website.

20.1.2. Diagram 770 (S2-2-51, see **Figure 20-1**) is used on the approach to a railway level crossing which is equipped with gates or barriers. This sign is also used at a tramway crossing if barriers are provided. Diagram 771 (S2-2-52, see **Figure 20-2**) is used in advance of open railway level crossings which have neither gates nor barriers.

May be used with a distance plate with or without an arrow pointing
to the left or right, an arrow pointing left or right or diagram 773

Figure 20-1 Diagram 770 (S2-2-51) **Figure 20-2** Diagram 771 (S2-2-52)
Level crossing with gate or barrier ahead Railway level crossing without gate or barrier ahead

20.1.3. Diagram 772 (S2-2-53, see **Figure 20-3**) is used in advance of open tramway crossings which have neither gates nor barriers. These signs should normally be sited at a distance from the crossing related to the 85th percentile speed of approaching vehicles, in accordance with **Appendix A**. See also **20.5** for guidance on the use of countdown markers and signing for queuing traffic.

20.1.4. Diagram 773 (S14-2-6, see **Figure 20-4**) should be used in advance of wig-wag signals to diagram 3014 (S14-2-5, see Chapter 6) at both railway and tramway level crossings. An arrow may be added to the sign pointing either to the left or to the right. An indication of distance may be added. The sign may be used only in combination with one of the warning signs described above, or with diagram 529 (S2-2-21, see **Figure 7-3**) or 558 (S2-2-46, see **Figure 13-1**) where wig-wag signals are used at an opening bridge or an airfield.

20.1.5. Diagram 774 (S2-6-4, see **Figure 20-5**) is used to indicate the location of a level crossing which has no gate or barrier. The same sign is used regardless of the number of tracks and at tramway as well as railway crossings.

20.1.6. Diagram 775 (S11-2-67, see **Figure 20-6**) is used at all automatic and open crossings. It should not be used at crossings with manually controlled barriers, nor at those which are user operated, unless specifically authorised in the Level Crossing Order. At automatic crossings, it should be placed on each primary and duplicate primary signal post. At open crossings, it should be mounted on both sides of the road, on or near the post carrying the sign to diagram 774.

May be used with a distance plate with or without an arrow pointing to the left or right, an arrow pointing left or right or diagram 773

Figure 20-3 Diagram 772 (S2-2-53)
Tramcar crossing ahead

May be used only in combination with diagram 529, 558, 770, 771 or 772. A distance, an arrow pointing to the left or right or both may be added

Figure 20-4 Diagram 773 (S14-2-6)
Stop at level crossing, tramcar crossing, opening bridge or airfield when lights show

May be used with diagram 602 when used with 778 or 778.1, or with signals to diagram 3014

Figure 20-5 Diagram 774 (S2-6-4)
Location of railway or tramway crossing without gate or barrier

May be used with signals to diagram 3014

Figure 20-6 Diagram 775 (S11-2-67)
Vehicular traffic must not stop within the area of a railway or tramway level crossing

20.1.7. Diagram 776 (S14-2-8, see **Figure 20-7**) is used at locally-monitored automatic open crossings on double-track lines, where two trains can arrive in quick succession. The sign should be sited on the left hand side of the road.

20.1.8. Diagram 777 (S14-2-8, see **Figure 20-8**) is used at all automatic crossings on double-track lines. The sign should be placed on or near each duplicate primary road traffic signal.

May be used with signals to diagram 3014. "TRAIN" may be varied to "TRAM"

Figure 20-7 Diagram 776 (S14-2-8)
Warning of another train or tramcar approaching the crossing

May be used with signals to diagram 3014. "TRAIN" may be varied to "TRAM"

Figure 20-8 Diagram 777 (S14-28)
Another train or tram passing

20.1.9. Diagrams 778 (S9-2-4, see **Figure 20-9**) and 778.1 (S9-2-5, see **Figure 20-10**) are used with the GIVE WAY sign to diagram 602 (S9-2-2) and not with signals to 3014. Special authorisation is required to use diagram 778.1 with the STOP sign to diagram 601.1.

May be used only in combination
with diagram 602 or 774

Figure 20-9 Diagram 778 (S9-2-4)
Open railway level crossing without light signals

May be used only in combination
with diagram 602 or 774

Figure 20-10 Diagram 778.1 (S9-2-5)
Open tramway crossing without light signals

20.2 Power cables

20.2.1. Diagram 779 (S2-2-54, see **Figure 20-11**) warns of a place where a road passes under an electrified overhead power cable. It must always be accompanied by a plate indicating the safe maximum height vehicle that can pass below the cable (see **Figure 20-12**, **Figure 20-13** & **Figure 20-14**). These signs are normally associated with overhead electric railway or tramway cables and should be used at all such crossings. Because of the high voltage of certain cables, it is very important to ensure that adequate warning is given even where cable heights are greater than 16'-6" (5.03 m).

May be used only in combination with the supplementary plates shown in figures 20-12, 20-13 and 20-14

Figure 20-11 Diagram 779 (S2-2-54) Electrified overhead cable ahead

20.2.2. Supplementary plates indicate this maximum safe height. The dimension may be varied and should show a height which is at least 2'-0" (600 mm) below the height of the overhead conductor for 25kV systems and 1'-6" (460 mm) for systems on lower voltages. At a crossing where the safe height is below 16'-6" (5.03 m), the height shown on the signs should be at least 1'-9" (530 mm) or 1'-3" (380 mm) respectively below the conductor and a load gauge to diagram 781 (S2-6-5, see **Figure 20-14**) erected at the safe height. In calculating the safe height, allowance should be made for the effect of the vertical profile of the carriageway on a road vehicle and its load. The height must be shown in both imperial and metric units. **Table 20-1** indicates the heights to be shown on the signs for different cable heights.

Safe height
16'-6" (5.0 m)

Figure 20-12 Safe height beneath cable (S2-2-54)

Safe height
15'-6" (4.7 m)
← 150 yds

Figure 20-13 Safe height beneath cable
in direction and at distance indicated (S2-2-54)

```
┌─────────────────────────────┐
│                             │
│       Safe height           │
│     15'-6" ( 4.7 m )        │
│       load gauge            │
│                             │
└─────────────────────────────┘
```

These plates may be used only in combination with diagram 779. The height may be varied.
The arrow may be reversed or omitted, and the distance may be varied or omitted

Figure 20-14 Load gauge and safe height beneath cable (S2-2-54)

20.2.3. The plates shown in **Figure 20-12** to **Figure 20-14** may be used only in combination with diagram 779 (see **Figure 20-11**). The height may be varied. The arrow may be reversed or omitted, and the distance may be varied or omitted.

Table 20-1 Load gauge sign criteria

Lowest hot weather height of contact wires above road		Height of gauge (diagram 781) and height to be shown on supplementary plate for different overhead line voltages				Signs to be used
		25000 volts		Less than 25000 volts		
Imperial	Metric	Imperial	Metric	Imperial	Metric	
18'-9"	5.71 m	16'-9"	5.1 m	17'-3"	5.2 m	Diagram 779 with **Figure 20-12** and **Figure 20-13**
18'-6"	5.64 m	16'-6"	5.0 m	17'-0"	5.1 m	
18'-3"	5.56 m	-	-	16'-9"	5.1 m	
18'-0"	5.49 m	-	-	16'-6"	5.0 m	
18'-3"	5.56 m	16'-6"	5.0 m	-	-	Load gauge (diagram 781) and diagram 779 with **Figure 20-14**
18'-0"	5.49 m	16'-3"	4.9 m	-	-	
17'-9"	5.41 m	16'-0"	4.8 m	16'-6"	5.0 m	
17'-6"	5.33 m	15'-9"	4.8 m	16'-3"	4.9 m	
17'-3"	5.26 m	15'-6"	4.7 m	16'-0"	4.8 m	
17'-0"	5.18 m	15'-3"	4.6 m	15'-9"	4.8 m	
16'-9"	5.10 m	15'-0"	4.5 m	15'-6"	4.7 m	
16'-6"	5.03 m	14'-9"	4.5 m	15'-3"	4.6 m	

20.3 Load gauge

20.3.1. The load gauge shown in diagram 781 (see **Figure 20-14**) gives an audible warning when the safe height beneath an overhead power cable is exceeded. The number of the bells may be varied. The bells may be of any colour provided each bell is of the same colour. It should always be used where the safe height is less than 16'-6" (5.03 m); see also **20.3.2**. A safe height less than 16'-6" is likely to be encountered only at private crossings. At such locations the gauge should be effective as speeds are low and users are familiar with the layout. The gauge is for use with power cables and not at low bridges over public highways, where speeds are likely to be higher and drivers less able to respond to the sound of the bells in time, or even to hear them at all from inside closed cabs.

20.3.2. The load gauge must be mounted on two posts coloured black and white in alternate horizontal bands, each band being not less than 250 mm nor more than 335 mm deep.

Diagram 779 (see **Figure 20-11**) with the supplementary plate shown in **Figure 20-14** should be used when a load gauge is installed.

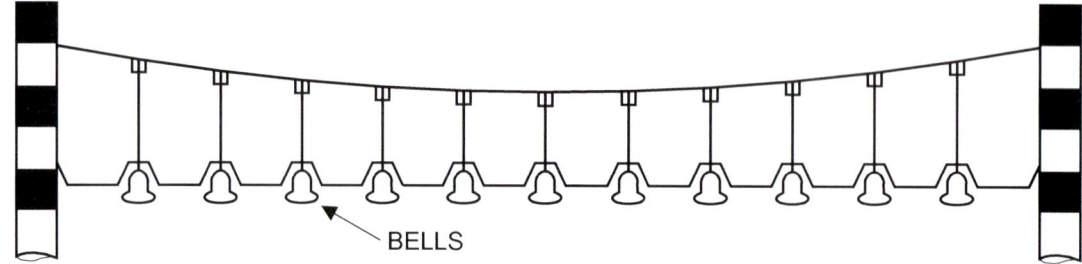

Figure 20-15 Diagram 781 (S2-6-5) Load gauge giving audible warning to drivers where vehicles exceed safe height under electrified overhead cables

20.4 Long vehicles

20.4.1. Diagram 782 (S2-2-55, see **Figure 20-16**) is used at railway or tramway level crossings where there is a risk of long or low vehicles grounding and causing an obstruction which might not be cleared before the next train or tram arrives at the crossing. It is necessary to consider both the approach profile and the relative levels of the running rails. For guidance on the use of this sign with hump bridges see **7.1**.

20.4.2. Diagrams 783 (S11-2-68, see **Figure 20-17**), 784.1 (S9-4-4, see **Figure 20-18**) and 785.1 (S11-2-69, see **Figure 20-19**) instruct drivers of long, low, large or slow vehicles to phone to obtain permission before crossing the railway. The smallest size of the sign to diagram 785.1 (25 mm x-height) is intended to be read only by a driver having alighted. A larger size will be required if it is necessary for the sign to be read from a moving vehicle. As non-compliance with the sign to diagram 784.1 could result in an accident or expose a driver to prosecution, it is essential that this group of signs is appropriately sized and properly maintained.

May be used with diagram 528, 783, 785.1, 786, a distance plate with or without an arrow pointing to the left or right or an arrow alone

Figure 20-16 Diagram 782 (S2-2-55) Risk of grounding at a railway or tramway level crossing or humped back bridge ahead

DRIVERS OF LONG LOW VEHICLES phone before crossing	DRIVERS OF LARGE OR SLOW VEHICLES phone before crossing

May be used with diagram 601.1, 782, 785.1, 786, 787 or 788

Figure 20-17 Diagram 783 (S11-2-68) Drivers of long low, large or slow vehicles must telephone to obtain permission before using a railway or tram crossing (Alternative types)

Drivers of LARGE or SLOW VEHICLES must phone and get permission to cross

LARGE means over 61'-6" (18.75 m) long or 9'-6" (2.9 m) wide or 44 tonnes total weight
SLOW means 5 mph or less

May be used with diagram 786, 787 or 788. "must phone" may be varied to "must use SOS phone"

Figure 20-18 Diagram 784.1 (S9-4-4)
Drivers of large or slow vehicles must stop and telephone before using a level crossing

The name of the crossing may be varied and displayed on any number of lines. "TO CONTACT RAILWAY" may be on one line, "RAILWAY" may be varied to "TRAM Co." and the telephone number varied. May be used with diagram 782 or 783

Figure 20-19 Diagram 785.1 (S11-2-69)
Name of level crossing and details of telephone number for contacting railway or tramway operator

20.4.3. Diagram 786 (S11-2-70, see **Figure 20-20**) indicates the place where a vehicle should wait while the driver telephones before or after crossing the railway line. A marking to diagram 1028.4 (with no accompanying legend, S7-4-6) may be used with the sign.

PARK HERE AND USE PHONE

PARK HERE AND USE PHONE AT CROSSING

May be used with diagram 782, 783, 784.1, 787, 788 or 1028.4. "AND USE PHONE" may be varied to "AND USE SOS PHONE" or "& USE SOS PHONE". The latter should be used only when plating an existing sign (see working drawing P 786)

Figure 20-20 Diagram 786 (S11-2-70) Parking place where large, slow or long vehicles should wait near a railway or tramway level crossing while the driver obtains permission by telephone to cross or confirms he or she has crossed

20.4.4. Diagrams 787 (S11-2-71, see **Figure 20-21**) and 788 (S11-2-72, see **Figure 20-22**) are used to indicate the location of the telephone. Diagram 788 is used only where this is not readily apparent.

Figure 20-21 Diagram 787 (S11-2-71)
Site of telephone or emergency telephone at or near a railway or tramway level crossing (Alternative types)

Figure 20-22 Diagram 788 (S11-2-72)
Direction to telephone or emergency telephone at or near a railway or tramway level crossing (Alternative types)

20.5 Countdown markers

20.5.1. Countdown markers to diagrams 789, 789.1 and 789.2 (S2-6-6, see **Figure 20-23**) may be used to emphasise the approach to a level crossing. They are intended to divide into equal lengths the distance between the first marker, with three bars, and the crossing. The first marker should be co-located with the warning sign to diagram 770, 771 or 772 (see **20.1**). Unlike the countdown markers on the approach to a junction, the bars do not represent intervals of 100 yards, as the warning sign will usually be less than 300 yards from the crossing. If the signs are duplicated on the off side of the road, for greater emphasis or to improve visibility, the slope of the bars is reversed.

20.5.2. Where queues sometimes extend upstream of the crossing warning signs, especially if the end of the queue might be hidden by a bend, queue warning signs might be necessary.

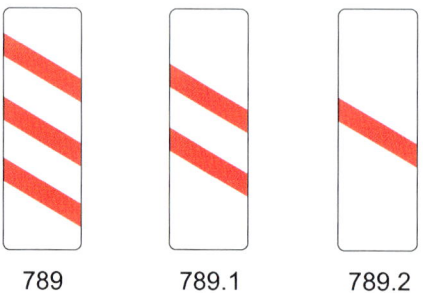

789   789.1   789.2

The signs are reversed when mounted on the off side

Figure 20-23 Countdown markers to railway or tramway level crossing (S2-6-6)

20.6 New crossings

20.6.1. Diagram 790 (S14-2-67, see **Figure 20-24**) is used following alteration of the method of control of a level crossing. In the case of a new installation, "CONTROL" should be omitted. The sign must be removed within three months of the date of completion of the works (Schedule 14 General Directions item 39). Guidance on the appropriate sizes for triangular warning signs and supplementary plates can be found in **Appendix A** and **Appendix B** respectively. Diagrams 774, 775, 777, 783 to 786 and 788 are prescribed in several sizes, the smallest being appropriate where approach speeds do not exceed 30 mph, and the largest where the national speed limit applies. For intermediate approach speeds, sizes should be proportioned accordingly, using the nearest prescribed size.

Figure 20-24 Diagram 790 (S14-2-67) New method of controlling traffic at a railway or tramway level crossing ahead

21.1 General

21.1.1. Diagram 950 (S2-2-26, see **Figure 21-1**) may be used to warn traffic of a place where a cycle route crosses or joins a road and is not controlled by traffic signals. Where cyclists emerge only from the left, the right hand sign should be used. If cycles cross the road, a plate "Cycles crossing" may be used; a distance and if appropriate an arrow may be added (i.e. if the cycle crossing is in a side road or another road). Details can be found on the working drawing (see **1.16**). Where cycles join the road but do not cross it, a distance plate (or distance plate with an arrow if the cycle route is in a side road) may be used. Where the junction is controlled by traffic signals, no warning sign is normally needed. If visibility of the signals is restricted, the appropriate sign is diagram 543 (see Chapter 6).

21.1.2. The version of diagram 950 for temporary situations has an associated plate "Child cycle tests" (S13-2-8, see **Figure 21-2**) which may be displayed when a children's cycle testing or training session is in progress. It must be used with diagram 950 and be removed when the session is completed. When a cycle rally or similar large event is in progress, the variant "Cycle event" may be used. An indication of the distance to the hazard may be included, and an arrow pointing to the left or to the right if the hazard is in another road.

May be used with a distance plate with or without an arrow pointing
to the left or right, an arrow alone or the supplementary plate below

Figure 21-1 Diagram 950 (S2-2-6, S13-2-8) Cycle route, race or test ahead

May be used only in combination with diagram 950. "tests" may be varied to "training".
"Child cycle tests" may be varied to "Cycle crossing", "Cycles crossing" or to "Cycle event".
A distance, an arrow or both may be added

Figure 21-2 Training or testing of child cyclists supplementary plate (S13-2-8)

22 REFUGE INDICATOR LAMPS

22.1 General

22.1.1. The purpose of the lamp is to indicate the presence of a refuge which might be obscured by other traffic, the brow of a hill or a bend. It is not normally necessary on refuges which carry lighting columns or traffic signals.

22.1.2. The beacon consists of an illuminated spherical globe conforming to the following requirements prescribed in S14-1-29 (regulation 46 in the Northern Ireland Regulations, where the dimensions are slightly different):

a) the globe shall be white;

b) it shall have a diameter of not less than 275 nor more than 335 mm; and

c) the height of the centre of the globe above the surface of the carriageway in the immediate vicinity shall be not less than 3800 mm nor more than 5000 mm.

22.1.3. The post supporting the lamp should, except as provided in **22.1.4**, be coloured grey or black, unless it is of aluminium, concrete or galvanised metal construction, in which case it may retain its natural colour (S14-6, General Direction 45(7)). Two white bands must be added, each band being between 275 and 335 mm in depth, separated by a gap of the same dimensions. The top white band should be between 275 and 335 mm below the white globe. The two white bands may be internally illuminated. See illustration of the complete refuge indicator lamp assembly in **Figure 22-1**.Signs to diagram 610 (S3-2-2, see Chapter 3) to indicate which side drivers should pass may be added.

22.1.4. When a lamp is placed on a street refuge or central reservation at a Zebra or Parallel crossing and yellow globes are also attached to the same post, the post from ground level up to the point where the yellow globes are attached must be coloured in alternate black and white horizontal bands. The lowest band must be black and be between 275 and 1000 mm deep, with the other bands being not less than 275 nor more than 335 mm deep. Above the point where the yellow globes are attached, the post should be coloured in accordance with **22.1.3**.

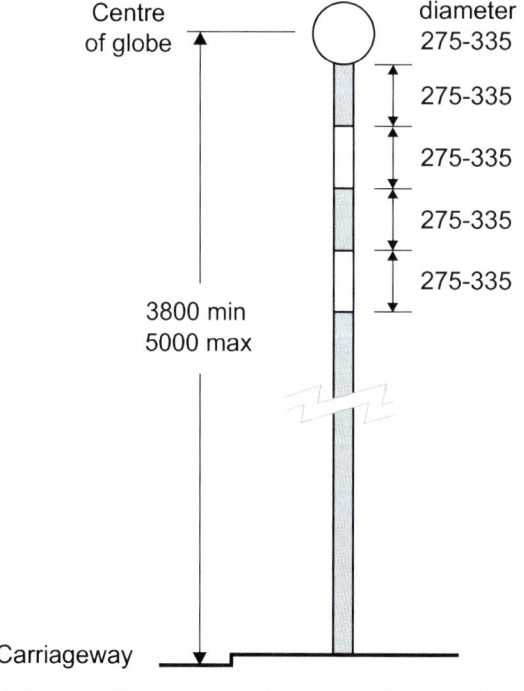

Figure 22-1 Refuge beacon (S14-1-29)

APPENDIX A

Table A-1 Sizes of warning signs and siting details

1	2	3	4
85th percentile speed of private cars (mph)	Height of triangular warning signs (mm)[3]	Minimum clear visibility distance (m)[4]	Distance of sign from hazard (m)[5]
Up to 20	600	45	45
21 to 30	600	60	45
31 to 40	750 (600)[1]	60	45-110
41 to 50	900 (750)[1]	75	110-180
51 to 60	1200 (900)[1]	90	180-245
Over 60	1200 (1500)[2]	105 (120)[2]	245-305[2]

NOTES

1. The smaller bracketed sizes shown in column 2 should be used only where special amenity considerations or physical constraints apply (see **1.8.2**). The minimum clear visibility distance specified in column 3 should not be reduced.

2. The 1500 mm size shown in column 2, and the largest visibility and siting distances in columns 3 and 4, should normally be used where the speed limit is 70 mph on dual three-lane or four-lane motorways or all-purpose roads with hard shoulders. In other circumstances the 1200 mm size should normally be used, with the 105 m minimum clear visibility distance (see **1.9.3** and **1.9.4**) shown in column 3 and the siting distance (see **1.9.1** and **1.9.2**) shown in column 4 (adjusted in accordance with Note 5 below). However, road safety considerations may require a larger size. The Regulations prescribe a 1500 mm size for most warning signs, which may be used on roads other than those described above.

3. **Table A-2** shows, in millimetres, the appropriate heights of the triangular warning signs and the diameters of regulatory signs that indicate the headroom of a bridge or other structure. For signs on the approach, the minimum clear visibility distance and the distance from the hazard shall be in accordance with the above table for all warning signs. The sign to diagram 530A when placed on the approach to a hazard is more likely to indicate an overhanging building or structure where the maximum size is 900 mm and 1200 mm respectively (see **Appendix B**) rather than to indicate a low bridge (see section **7**).

Table A-2 Sizes and siting details for low headroom signs

Diagram number and sign location	85th percentile speed of private cars (mph)			
	Up to 30	31 to 40	41 to 50	Over 50
530A mounted on structure	900	1200	1500	1800
530A on approach	750	900	1200	1500
531.1 on approach	750	900	1200	1500
532.2	750	900	1200	1500
532.2A	900	1200	1500	1800
532.3 (centre of arch)	750	900	1200	1500
532.3 (side of arch)	600	750	900	1200
532.3A (centre of arch)	900	1200	1500	1800
532.3A (side of arch)	750	900	1200	1500
629.2 mounted on structure	600	750	900	1200
629.2 on approach	600	750	900	1200
629.2A mounted on structure	750	900	1200	1500
629.2A on approach	750	900	1200	1500

NOTES

1. For further guidance on clear visibility distance, see **1.9.3** and **1.9.4**. Siting also needs to take account of the location of other signs (e.g. advance direction signs) to ensure that one sign does not obstruct the sight line to another. Provision of a new sign might sometimes require the relocation of an existing one.

2. For further guidance on sign siting, see **1.9.1** and **1.9.2**. Where a range is quoted for siting distance in column 4, progressively larger figures should be used for 85th percentile speeds towards the higher end of the speed range, to compensate for the greater braking distance. Braking distance will also be affected by gradients, and siting distances may need to be increased on steep hills, e.g. an increase of 50% might be made for a 10% descent. Special considerations apply to the signs listed below:

(i) When used on single carriageway roads:

Diagram 563, when indicating "Blind summit" or "Hidden dip", might need to be placed further from the hazard than shown in column 4 of the first table to allow for a hidden vehicle approaching at speed

(ii) When used on high-speed dual carriageway roads:

Diagram 510 "Roundabout ahead" – see **2.4.2**

Diagram 520 "Dual carriageway ends ahead" – see **5.1**

Diagram 521 "Two-way traffic" – see **5.1**

(iii) When used on any road:

Diagram 522 "Two-way traffic on route crossing ahead" – see **5.2.2**

Diagram 558 "Low-flying aircraft" – see **13.1.2**

3. The combined metric/imperial height restriction warning triangle (diagram 530A) incorporated into a directional sign or the sign to diagram 818.5 (see **Figure 7-9** and Appendix D in Chapter 7) is 30 stroke widths in height. The combined metric/imperial height restriction roundel (diagram 629.2A) incorporated into a directional sign or a sign to diagram 818.4 (see **Figure 7-2** and Appendix D in Chapter 7) is 30 stroke widths in diameter. The table below sets out recommended x-heights and corresponding triangle heights and roundel diameters for the signs to diagrams 818.4 and 818.5, appropriate to various 85th percentile speeds. The dimension in brackets applies where motorways and all-purpose dual carriageway roads have three or more lanes per carriageway. For appropriate x-heights for directional

signs, see Appendix A in Local Transport Note 1/94 'The Design and Use of Directional Informatory Signs', available from TSO or www.gov.uk/government/collections/local-transport-notes.

Table A-3 Recommended x-heights for signs to diagrams 818.4 and 818.5 (S12-28-22 & 23)

85th percentile speed of private cars (mph)	x-height (mm)	Triangle height / roundel diameter (mm)
Up to 20	60	450
21 to 30	80	600
31 to 40	100	750
41 to 50	120	900
51 to 60	160	1200
61 to 70	200	1500
70 mph speed limit	240 (300)	1800 (2250)

NOTES

1. The height or diameter of the triangular or circular roundel shown above is based upon 30 stroke widths, the most common size. For S12-20-25 or 27 (structural weight limit or prohibition of vehicles carrying dangerous goods), this reduces to 24 sw.

2. 85th percentile speed measurement is dealt with in TA 22 'Vehicle speed measurement on all-purpose roads' in Volume 5 of DMRB (see **1.5.1**). The "dry weather spot speed" should be used. This is the speed only exceeded by only 15% of the cars.

Table B-1 Sizes of supplementary plates

Diagram No. (TSRGD ref)	Description	x-height or plate size (mm) appropriate to the triangle heights shown (see Appendix A)				
		600[1]	750[1]	900	1200[2]	1500[3]
502 (S2-6-1)	STOP 'x' yds	62.5	75	100	125	-
503 (S2-6-1)	GIVE WAY 'x' yds	62.5	75	100	125	-
511 (S2-3-1)	REDUCE SPEED NOW	62.5	75	100	125/150	200
513.1A (S2-2-7 to 12)	Adverse camber	50/62.5	75	100	125	150
513.2 (S2-3-2 & S13-4-2)	Maximum speed advised	50*/62.5	75	100	125	-
(S2-2-13 to 15)	Single file traffic	50/62.5	75	100	125	150
(S2-2-13 & 14)	Single track road	50/62.5	75	100	-	-
(S2-2-18 & 19)	Low gear now	50/62.5	75	100	125	150
(S2-2-8 to 12, 18, 19 & 39)	Keep in low gear	50/62.5	75	100	125	150
(S2-2-18 & 19)	Low gear for 'x' miles	50/62.5	75	100	125	150
530.1 (S2-5-1)	Overhanging building (when used with diagram 530)	50*/62.5	75	100	-	-
530.1 (S2-5-1)	Overhanging building (when used with diagram 530A)	-	50*/62.5	75	100	
531.2 (S2-5-2)	ARCH BRIDGE High vehicles use middle of road	-	75	100	125/150	-
543.1 (S14-2-29)	Part time signals	50/62.5	75	100	125	150
(S2-2-25)	School	50/62.5	75	100	125/150	-
(S2-2-25)	Patrol	62.5/75	100	125	150	-
(S2-2-25)	Playground	50/62.5	75	100	125/150	-
(S2-2-23 & 25)	No footway for 'x' yds	50/62.5	75	100	125/150	-
(S2-2-24)	Disabled people	50/62.5	75	100	125/150	-
(S2-2-25)	Disabled children	50/62.5	75	100	125/150	-
547.8 (S14-2-31)[4]	Humped crossing	50/62.5	75	100	125	
548.1A (S14-2-41)	When lights show 'x' yds	50/62.5	75	100	125	150
(S2-2-35)	Horse-drawn vehicles and animals	50*/62.5	75	100	-	-
(S2-2-34)	Farm traffic	50/62.5	75	100	125/150	150
(S13-2-4)	Ice	62.5/75	100	125	150	200
	Snowdrifts	62.5	75	100	125	150
(S2-2-42)	Soft verges for 'x' miles	50*/62.5	75	100	125	150
(S2-2-43)	Humps for 'x' miles	50	-	-	-	-

Diagram No. (TSRGD ref)	Description	x-height or plate size (mm) appropriate to the triangle heights shown (see Appendix A)				
		600[1]	750[1]	900	1200[2]	1500[3]
(S2-2-43)	Humps for 'x' yards in the direction indicated	50*/62.5	75	100	125	-
(S2-2-43)	Hump 'x' yards in the direction indicated	50*/62.5	75	100	125	-
(S2-2-46)	Gliders	50/62.5	75	100	125/150	150
(S2-2-56, 13-2-7)	Accident	62.5	75	100	125/150	200
563.1 (S14-2-7)	FIRE STATION STOP when lights show (x-height of lower case legend)	62.5	75	100	100	-
(S18-3)	For 'x' miles	50/62.5	75	100	125/150	200
572 (S2-5-5)	'x' yds (when used with diagram 530A or 531.1)	-	50/62.5	75	100	125/150
(S2-2)	'x' yds (when used with other warning signs)	50/62.5	75	100	125/150	200
572 (S2-5-5)	Distance and direction to hazard (when used with diagram 530A or 531.1)	-	50/62.5	75	100	125/150
(S2-2)	Distance and direction to hazard (when used with other warning signs)	50/62.5	75	100	125/150	200
(S2-2-8 to 14, 20 & 22)	Oncoming vehicles in middle of road	50/62.5	75	100	125	150
(S2-2-49)	Slow lorries for 'x' miles	50/62.5	75	100	125/150	200
(S2-2-50)	Queues likely	50/62.5	75	100	125/150	200
773 (S14-2-6)	STOP when lights show (x-height of lower case legend)	62.5	75	100	125	-
778 (S9-2-4)	Train symbol (plate size)	440 x 420	550 x 525	660 x 630	660 x 630	-
778.1 (S9-2-5)	Tram symbol (plate size)	480 x 300	600 x 375	720 x 450	720 x 450	-
(S2-2-54)	Safe height	50/62.5	75	100	125	-
(S2-2-54)	Safe height at distance and in direction indicated	50/62.5	75	100	125	-
(S2-2-54)	Safe height and load gauge	50/62.5	75	100	125	-
817.2 (S2-3-3)	Escape lane ahead	50*/62.5	75	100	125	125
(S2-2-26, S13-2-8)	Child cycle tests	50*/62.5	75	100	-	-
7009.1 (S13-4-3)	Skid risk and maximum advised speed of 20 mph	50*/62.5	75	100	125	-

NOTES

1. For the 600 mm and 750 mm size triangles, the smaller x-height, where more than one is shown, is appropriate if the 85th percentile speed is 20 mph or less. Where a 50 mm x-height is marked with an asterisk, this is the standard size for 85th percentile speeds up to 30 mph.

2. For the 1200 mm size triangle, the larger x-height, where more than one is shown, should be used on dual carriageway roads where the national speed limit applies or on single carriageway roads where greater emphasis is required.

3. As a 1500 mm size sign is sometimes used in place of a 1200 mm sign (see **Appendix A**, **Table A-1**, note 2), x-heights for supplementary plates used in these circumstances are quoted even though that particular sign may not be used on motorways or all-purpose dual carriageways with grade separated junctions. The larger x-height, where more than one is shown, should be used on dual carriageway roads where the national speed limit applies or on single carriageway roads where greater emphasis is required.

4. The larger signs are intended for use on main roads when an arrow has been added to the plate indicating a humped pedestrian crossing in the minor road leading from the junction ahead.

5. Although permitted by the Regulations, diagram 530A is unlikely to be used with the supplementary plates to diagrams 572 and 573 (see section **7**).

LIST OF FIGURES

INDEX